Copyright © 2016 by James Sandfield
All rights reserved.
ISBN: 1523372680
ISBN-13: 978-1523372683

I think this is a fantastic book. I have to be honest enough to say that at first thought "a book on standards: how boring can this be?" I was positively and amazingly surprised. It is very easy to read with good and relevant examples. I will really encourage my leadership team to read this.

Vice President, Fortune 100 company

What problem are you trying to solve?

Table of Contents

Table of Contents 3
List of Diagrams 6
Foreword 7
Preface 9
INTRODUCTION 12
   Don't be a tool head 12
   The Swedish chicken salad game 13
   Easier and more enjoyable 17
CHAPTER 1: WHAT TO DO AND WHY 20
   Today's standards 20
   Bucket loads of benefits 23
   Benefits of standards 28
CHAPTER 2: WHAT IS LEAN? 29
   Lean is a strategy 29
   7 Wastes in the process 33
   7 Values for the customer 37
   Some "standard" definitions to help 43
   Last definition (I promise) 44
CHAPTER 3: FUNDAMENTALS TO LEARN 45
   12 principles to guide you 45
   PDCA in one minute 47
   Leadership success factors 49
   Customer demand 50

What problem are you trying to solve?

Try before you buy	52
Pick up the pen game	53

CHAPTER 4: "PLAN" WHAT TO DO 62

Empower a group of people	62
Break paradigms not people	63
You are not the expert	65
Establish a goal for improvement	68
Why is seven(ty) the right challenge?	70
SMART goals	72
Summary of Principles that "Plan"	73

CHAPTER 5: "DO" IMPROVEMENT 75

Understand the ways of working	75
Observation, not a guessing game	76
Golden rules of Gemba	78
Find a better sequence for the task	80
Rearranging for the better	83
Work Combination Charts	87
Make the workplace easy	93
Spring cleaning for the right reason	95
Stationery not stationary	98
Find a great way to follow the task	101
Summary of Principles that "Do"	104

CHAPTER 6: "CHECK" ACHIEVEMENT 107

Test the proposed way of working	107
Evaluate the test	110
Checking your fax	113

What problem are you trying to solve?

Build consensus	115
Employee scores not robot wars	116
Red tape disintegrates	117
Summary of Principles that "Check"	118
CHAPTER 7: "ACT" BY IMPLEMENTING	**121**
Establish the new standard	121
A tidy garage	122
A car without a petrol gauge	124
Train the new standard	125
Manage the new standard	128
Want to know a secret?	133
The key in a keystroke	136
Summary of Principles that "Act"	137
CONCLUSION	**140**
Banish reductionism	140
A letter from John Shook	143
Standards work	148
Coming soon	151
About the author	152

What problem are you trying to solve?

List of Diagrams

DIAGRAM
A: Standardized Work without effective standards in place
B: Standardized Work with effective standards in place
C: The 7 wastes tackled by lean thinking (and standards)
D: The 7 values enhanced by lean thinking (and standards)
E: Factors which ensure reliable supply
F: 12 Principles to follow when solving problems and saving effort
G: PDCA cycle
H: Pick up the pen observation template
I: Pick up the pen new process to test
J: Pick up the pen new standard
K: Proposed reasons for high or low performance
L: A watch from memory and from observation
M: Template for 5-10 minutes of observation
N: A typical airport experience for any passenger wanting to fly
O: A new layout for a new experience
P: Faxed orders Work Combination Chart (before **4TH PRINCIPLE**)
Q: Faxed orders Work Combination Chart (after **4TH PRINCIPLE**)
R: Calculation of how long customers wait for faxed orders
S: Spring cleaning incorrectly with the 5S method
T: Stationery cupboard living up to its new standard
U: Faxed orders with a visual solution
V: Building confidence with trials within your process
W: Faxed orders: Evaluation of improvement
X: A slightly excessive standard on how to use the garage
Y: PDCA and its continuous relationship with SDCA

What problem are you trying to solve?

Foreword

When James approached me saying, "I have a great idea I will write a book about standards and standardized work", I was a bit surprised. He followed up with a statement that "there are few to no books about either of these", I checked, he is right, so I continued listening.

I already know that standards and standardized work are the most important tools in lean as they examine how people optimize processes; so I looked forward to reading and making suggestions with regards to this book.

Use the methods described within this book and you will find huge potential to decrease the amount of time a task will take to fulfill. The capacity released should be used to either fuel further improvement or it should be used to create more value to the customer. This increased value could be an extra service provided or another product produced without increasing the resources needed to fulfill that extra product or service. Insourcing of activities, normally conducted outside your organization, can also be an option.

Nevertheless many examples of standards and standardized work have been misused. They have been used to cut personnel costs, leading to a disengaged workforce. You should never forget that this strategy does not only put application of standards and engagement of employees at risk, but the entire transformation journey of turning your organization into a lean enterprise will also be at risk.

When applying standards it is the duty of the management and the lean

What problem are you trying to solve?

experts to take care of the people involved, they need to be treated respectfully. More than all other lean tools, standards and standardized work need to be well defined in terms of application; what problem you are trying to solve and how to use the expected gained capacity. In many cases the creativity of management in using this capacity is quite limited. Also you should never underestimate the role that Human Resources plays in supporting people, as their jobs and roles change, during the adoption of standards and standardized work.

I believe that within this book you will find a very logical and easy way to understand how to approach standards and standardized work and the key elements you should follow to be successful.

The approaches, pitfalls and benefits described above are well covered in this book. Use these methods, be successful and do not misuse standards to give lean a bad name – remember what problem you are trying to solve!

Oliver Frohns
January 2016

What problem are you trying to solve?

Preface

I wrote this book, not because I know the answer, but because I want to bring clear guidance, to everyone, on how to solve a problem. It is not important to show myself as the expert with the knowledge; trying a few lofty quotes, introducing some recycled evidence or even inventing a new model. What I want to do is explain how to use standards and standardized work to eliminate too much effort.

I have consolidated 10 years of practical lean application, across 25 years of business experience. If you work in a small business, a global enterprise or anything between, I have worked in a similar range of companies. I cleaned offices when I was at school, worked with around 100 companies in my early 20s and then settled down with 2 global leaders, of their respective industries, for the last 20 years.

At the turn of the millennium, I decided that I should be a leader and started changing my leadership style; I decided to evolve beyond the concept of manager.

After a few years, I thought I was making good progress; according to my director, my peers and my colleagues they agreed. I was starting to think that I had transformed from manager to leader.

However, a lean consultant approached me about 10 years ago and the following transpired.

What problem are you trying to solve?

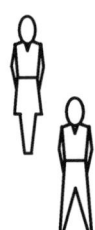
Consultant: "James, why do you tell your people what to do?"

Naturally, I could not miss an opportunity to show how years of experience had put me in such a knowledgeable position. "I know what they do, I know the difficult contracts. I help with the answer."

Her reply was more inquisitive than I anticipated "how many hours a week do you do that person's job?" as she pointed to one of my colleagues.

"1 hour a week" was my confident reply; I had helped them with a difficult issue only a couple of days before.

Consultant: "How long do they do their job?"

"40 hours a week" was my reply and to show how brilliant I was, I even added to the statement "there are 10 people doing that role, so that makes 400 hours."

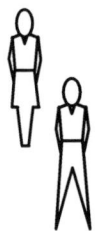
Consultant: "If they do their job 400 hours a week, and you do it 1 hour a week, why do you tell them what to do?"

No answer came from my lips.

I thought about this overnight, and resigned as Head of Finance Operations in a multi-billion organization the next day. Then I started learning, I had to find out how she could prove me wrong.

What problem are you trying to solve?

I have written this book in an open discussion style. This allows you, the reader, to absorb and reflect on the points of view given. Follow the recommendations within this book, with your own insight, and you can be successful.

Through the Joy of Standards, you will help your organization move from spending endless hours on simple everyday tasks to empowering everyone to spend time on tasks that customer's value.

Remember success is learning from your own experimentation not from blindly following my instructions and always, always remember: what problem you are trying to solve!

Enjoy reading the book, comments for improvement are welcome.

James Sandfield **FCCA MSc**
January 2016

What problem are you trying to solve?

INTRODUCTION

Don't be a tool head

Having picked this book, I guess you have a problem you would like to solve. I hope that the problem is a task or series of tasks in your organization that are taking too much effort to complete.

You or your colleagues have previously seen that staying late and securing more resource can be solutions to the challenges within the task, but these solutions are only reactive. So to solve the problem, you train, impose standards, introduce incentives, automate, offshore and sub-contract. The problem only comes back or your bottom line seems to shrink, even when you use automation and cheaper resource. Perhaps a better approach to standards is the solution?

I would like you to ask yourself: is this true? Surely you can get to where you want to go, without needing to learn something new. The answer will be no. Think about it, you have the problem from the thinking you have applied previously, so the solution cannot come from the same thinking. After all, Einstein said "insanity is doing the same thing over and over again and expecting different results".

WARNING: If you apply standards and standardized work as a solution to problems, which do not have too much effort; you will not achieve anything noteworthy.

What problem are you trying to solve?

The Swedish chicken salad game

Let me show you a typical problem, with too much effort, through a small exercise written on a train from Stockholm to Copenhagen.

How many chicken salads did I need at my workshop in Stockholm?

The answer was a bit more problematic than you would think. Play along with me. Put your hand up to your ear, like you are on the telephone, and count the following with your other hand:

CHICKEN SALAD:

It took someone three attempts before they were confident about the answer to give to the caterer over the telephone. Did you have a similar problem? How long did it take you to have a definitive answer, are you now going back to the list to double check? Holding a book and holding an imaginary telephone, may have seemed a bit silly, wherever you are reading this book, but that was similar to the real situation encountered one day in a workshop.

Imagine, if it only took 3 seconds to count the list with certainty that your answer will always be right. This is precisely the type of problem solved with the Joy of Standards; too much effort was being applied to the task.

What problem are you trying to solve?

How about I change your 10 seconds, be honest with yourself, and turn the time to count into 3 seconds with an even longer list of chicken salads required.

Should I re-train you? How many times have you counted to 19 in your lifetime, let's say 10,000. Maybe I could test you, can you count to 19? Yes and you have passed the test. No and you have failed the interview, I do not want you.

So why, as I know you are competent, can you not count the chicken salads in 3 seconds? Easy answer, I will put an incentive in place. Count in 3 seconds or less to get a bonus. Count in 4 or 5 seconds stay late after work until all your work is done. Count in 6 seconds or more then you are fired. Sounds similar to many incentive schemes I have encountered. Does it also resonate with you?

Unfortunately, the most likely outcome to an incentive scheme like this will be a mixture of creative reporting, arguments and cheating, almost everyone can justify their bonus, but almost none of the orders will be completed accurately in less than 6 seconds.

Eureka! We live in the Digital Age not the Stone Age. I will ask some developers to invent an App to read the chicken salad orders, it will only take €100,000 and 6 months and then I will never have the chicken salad counting problem again. One minor problem; why do I need an expensive investment for a simple problem? Who says that the App will always receive a nice neat list of chicken salad requests in the format needed (the real chicken salad orders went onto the margin of the order sheet).

What problem are you trying to solve?

Also, I am not sure an App can cope with all scenarios (salad without oil anyone?); neither can any automated solution whether it is the world's most powerful supercomputer or whether it is a simple bar code reader. I am not saying Information Technology does not have a role in standards, I am just saying that it is better to eliminate problems before automating processes.

I could outsource the chicken salad counting; find a low cost provider, who, if they receive all orders by 10am will send them to the caterer by 11am. It does not matter that it takes longer to provide the information to the outsource provider, what matters is that I no longer have the waste of counting, someone else has this waste.

Similar problems can apply to outsourcing and automation. It is often difficult for these solutions to cope with rapidly changing customer requirements, exceptions and variable requests. Both of these solutions can create problems for employees and customers because they are enabled through much needed definition and control. Automation uses an IT system and outsourcing uses a Service Level Agreement, both controls become constraints and can therefore lead to frustration.

If training, incentives, automation and outsourcing have limitations then there is a need to apply better thinking; this is called lean thinking. Lean thinking tells you that when a task takes too much effort, you should eliminate as much of that effort as possible and the tools to use are standards and standardized work. Even better, training, incentives, automation and outsourcing are still appropriate, and can be successful, when they follow or accompany lean thinking.

Within this book, I will put forward that standards and standardized work often eliminate 70% of the effort within a process. I will also ask you to use

What problem are you trying to solve?

your people and their brains to find solutions. It is then that you should consider how best to facilitate the new process. These processes will be dynamic people led solutions, enabled by the right amount of training, incentives, automation and outsourcing.

You will build an optimum approach;
    For your employees (as you will value their opinions).
    Your customers (as your process is coping with changing requirements).
    Your organization (as you minimize locked-in costs).

The chicken salad is a good example of a challenge that does not need a huge investment; it just needs some brain power. Try a better process, with the same people and same ink and paper technology.

Each "bar and gate" tally represents five. So your answer in 3 seconds is….?

CHICKEN SALAD: ||||/ ||||/ ||||/ ||||/ ||

The alternative is to carry on as you are. Aim for 5-10% improvement every year, hit something just below 5% and then wonder why your projects fail to deliver any significant change which lasts. Even worse, you know your people and customers think the process is deteriorating.

What problem are you trying to solve?

Easier and more enjoyable

Important features exist within standards. The first is that they must be easier to do than the old way: for everyone, not just the person improving the task. Why should anyone follow the new solution if it makes their life more difficult? The new solution has to be the clear choice of everyone who is expected to participate in the new process. They have to feel and see the benefit.

The new solution also has to be more relevant than the old alternative, as human beings we cannot expect people to be robots. If you make a solution which constrains your people to a mind-numbing experience, then one of five things will happen:

1. Boredom will distract your people and they will pursue more interesting activities like organizing next weekend's trip to the countryside.
2. Procrastination, as people avoid the task. Anything will be better than doing this task, they will find something else to do when the opportunity arises; they will leave this task until another day, even if it is needed today.
3. Poor quality, as people take short cuts to meet expectations but happily avoid key activities within the task; have you ever seen a process completed by someone that knew what they were doing but could not understand why rework was required? Reliable high quality should be part of a process and the need to inspect should cease to happen.
4. Reputation problems as people compromise your brand values. A standard should be the best known way to complete the task safely for

employees and customers. Avoiding the standard will therefore be compromising one of these. Organizations that are effective in using standards have good reputations. Their standards need to be used, followed and improved: not just certified and put on a book shelf.
5. Overtime and unexpected labor costs as people ignore the new solution: instead of following an imperfect answer, from their perspective, they will invent their own version, even if that version takes more effort; at least it is interesting to them and makes them feel like they made a difference.

Other important features of standards are that tasks should be easily repeatable; it needs to look like a child could have designed or discovered the solution. This is important; if it is that simple, then it has probably eliminated the problems within the old process. Repeatability is also an indicator that the new solution will be easy to train; an important success factor is that everyone can do the task without the need for excessive training. Training is important but spending time and money un-necessarily is not good business.

The last feature is that new standards should almost always cost nothing to implement: expensive solutions take time and can limit future options for improvement. Money is an interesting dilemma; it is often thought that you cannot revolutionize or rescue processes without it, but, are you trying to buy your way out of one problem only to find a new one?

When you only find investment is the solution, then you have probably automated the waste or you have delayed potential benefits; usually a combination of both occurs. Even worse, ever buy something new and think that you must use it or you will feel it was a waste of money, what happens 3, 6 or 9 months later? You stop using it and start using something simpler

What problem are you trying to solve?

instead, it does not matter that the solution had a payback of 2, 3 or 4 years. It worked for the time that it was used.

Easier, reliable, repeatable and not expensive to implement; now that you know what standards and standardized work solutions aim to do (on effort reduction) and the "chicken salad" features they show within solutions, you need to learn how to do this. First you need to learn an important answer to a basic question: what are the benefits of standards?

What problem are you trying to solve?

CHAPTER 1: WHAT TO DO AND WHY

Today's standards

Standards are a fundamental part of standardized work, and this is not just deconstruction of the phrase. So is this another way of management managing people and not leadership leading people? The answer is yes, if you stick with the traditional perceptions regarding the benefits of standards.

I say benefits, but really, these are the confused beliefs around standards. These confusions usually start with the following statement: "if it is defined as a standard, then you know what everybody is doing. If you know what everybody is doing, then you know that they are doing everything correctly."

A quick test: which standards do you follow? Are there any what-so-ever, be honest with yourself, for the job you were recruited to do. Are these standards for this job, or are these standards for administrative tasks that apply to many people?

Let me ask you, for the standards you listed, are you trained in these processes until you have the confidence that you can perform the task accurately? Can you find the standard in a written or electronic form within five seconds? When was the last time you looked at the standard to guide you in doing this task? When was the standard last improved? Were you involved in that improvement or was it communicated to you by people who know best?

If all of your answers to my previous questions are as follows, you know the benefits of standards.

What problem are you trying to solve?

I follow standards for all the important parts of my job
(I know what is expected from me).
Training on the standard was in advance, effective and appropriate
(I know I can do my job properly).
I feel confident that the standard produces the right result
(I know I do not create problems for colleagues, customers or my organization).
I thought about how to improve the standard when I followed it
(my contribution is valued and essential to keep my organization competitive).
My manager supports 100% use of the standard by seeing it used
(I know my manager cares about me and my success).
Every person who follows this standard produces the same reliable output
(even when I am away, I do not need to worry about problems when colleagues follow the standard).
I have someone in my team to turn to if I cannot follow the standard
(I know that someone is here to help me, with high quality support, at a time which ensures my customer's requirement is not delayed).
The standard has improved multiple times recently
(I know that the standard is getting better and that this is good).

And last, but possibly the most controversial:

The last time I read the standard was on the day I performed the task
(I know I am following the most recent version of the standard. This is from a good recent memory not a vague memory which could contain misunderstanding or out-of-date knowledge).

What problem are you trying to solve?

In organizations that live with the benefits of standards, that was their list of answers. If you do not have all of these answers; there is opportunity for you to learn more about the benefits of standards.

Unfortunately a standard is usually the written best practice of the process, reviewed occasionally and followed by someone, sometimes, but no-one can recall who that person is or when they followed it. I have seen standards that are 10 years old. I have seen employees unable to find the standard when I asked to see it. Lastly, there are also standards which are best practices; but they cannot be followed because this is the ideal, not an expectation of reality.

As this is the situation in so many places today, then no wonder people do not like standards, they see them as how to restrict, control and manage them into doing the task in a way that others see fit and if they are caught not following the standard then they are at fault, even worse, if not following the standard resulted in a problem, then they are fired.

How about understanding the Joy of Standards and an ability to articulate their features before embarking on optimizing with standards and standardized work?

What problem are you trying to solve?

Bucket loads of benefits

To have the Joy of Standards you need to understand why standards are beneficial. What type of benefits they are and why they occur. By having this understanding, you will implement them, where you need them, for the right processes.

By empowering the people that do the task to define the standards they need, you respect their opinion and you bring their knowledge into the process. After all, it is their 40 hours a week that performs the task, with the local conditions and requirements, not a 40 hour a year expert who used to do the job 3 years ago.

Your business, will no longer need to worry that when one person leaves they take the knowledge with them, it will;

a. No longer complain that people with the right skills are not on the open market.
b. Have the knowledge in the walls of your organization, not in the legs of its people.
c. Be able to train new staff to a competent level (according to the challenges expected within their role).
d. Be able to have effective people with less training time (typically 70% less).

These are all softer benefits of standards, hard to track and hard to put onto a Profit & Loss account. They depend on factors often outside your control, the decision about employment is both a business requirement and a personal

What problem are you trying to solve?

choice, what you need are benefits that are clear to the customer and to your employer.

Immediate performance improvement when you adopt a standard is possible. If you take twenty people doing the same process in different ways, some people will have some techniques that could benefit others. By empowering a group of people on behalf of the twenty to look into defining a standard, you allow them to discover the current best way to perform the process at a high quality, you adopt many of the benefits that were previously held by a few.

Even better, continuous improvement happens faster when you have a standard. Imagine twenty people all following their own version of a standard; one person has an idea and one person benefits. Now imagine the same twenty people following the same version of the standard; one person has an idea and twenty people benefit, in fact the opportunity for benefits is not just twenty fold, it is twenty times more frequent ideas benefitting twenty people's standard. Now that's what I call continuous improvement (which can impact the bottom line).

The perfect day at work can happen for the employer, employee and customer when pragmatic standards are in place and working. Employers know which resource and how much resource is needed for a given set of customer requests. Employees know how to do the task and to what quality it should be completed. Customers receive their promises on time and to the required level.

In fact, standards set your people free to concentrate on the things that matter to the customer; is it better quality, is it more efficient ways of working or is it innovative solutions to delight them? These growth opportunities are the

What problem are you trying to solve?

competitive edge that comes from excellent task execution; they make a difference to your top line.

The test to give yourself, after all this advice is: can you explain the benefits of standards to any employee from any colleague to any leader? If you can, then you can benefit from having standards in your organization. If you cannot, then why would you optimize a process with the Joy of Standards, when you cannot explain the benefits of following standards.

The below diagram shows the reliance processes place on the partnership of standardized work (improving processes) and standards (managing processes).

DIAGRAM A: Standardized work without effective standards in place

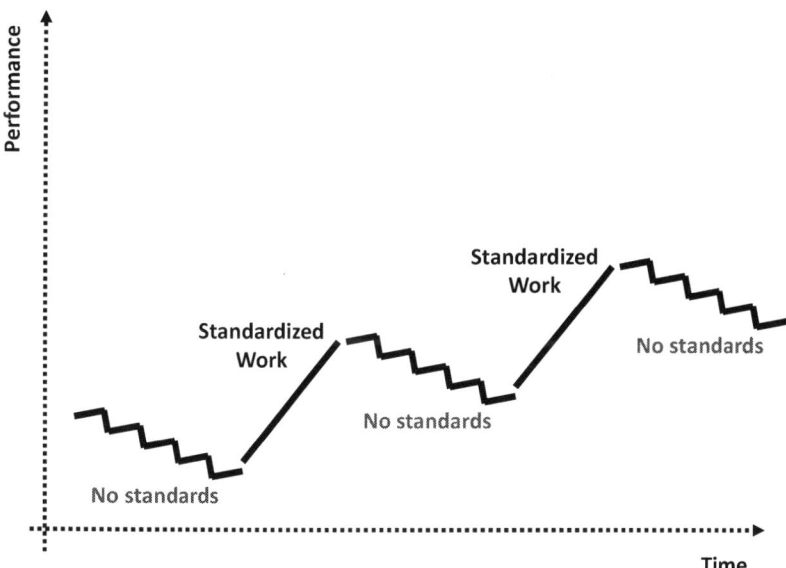

No standards + standardized work = improvement which falls back

What problem are you trying to solve?

When you do not have standards in place, each standardized work improvement makes performance rise for a short period of time. The old ways return; changes needed from a process, customer or employee perspective are not acted on.

Eventually the task is not able to perform at the level required and a new standardized work project is required. A project mindset is kept; there is no need for continuous improvement. Improvement will be reactive and hopefully this will be enough. Usually it is, leaders keep their bonuses, employees are downsized and shareholders receive inconsistent returns; not the best business strategy.

If you want the true benefit of standardized work, eliminating 70% of the effort from your tasks and keeping this benefit, then you must start by establishing, using and improving standards.

Standards need to become the accepted and repeated way of working in your organization; they are the foundations of improvement for which your organization will rely on.

This is why Taiichi Ohno, the man credited with creating the most effective lean organization in the world (Toyota), is quoted as saying "without standards there can be no improvement".

I happen to agree, and I hope that you are starting too as well. The graph that follows shows why standards and standardized work are harmonious and indisputable as the strategy to follow for improving processes.

What problem are you trying to solve?

DIAGRAM B: Standardized work with effective standards in place

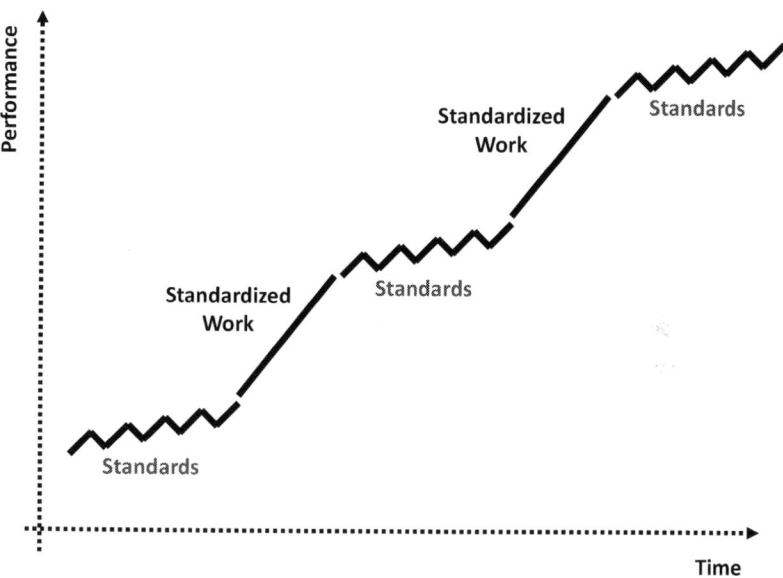

Standards + standardized work = competitive advantage

Each time a standard encounters an issue; your people will act and improve the standard. Standardized work builds on these continually improving standards by leveraging the continuous improvement mindset within your people and challenging them to take the process to a new level of performance. Your people will deliver and they will manage the new standard so they can make further improvements. This process will never end as it is a journey not a destination.

What problem are you trying to solve?

Benefits of standards

Test your knowledge; can you explain (to anyone) the benefits of standards? Can you do this under two minutes without any jargon?

	BENEFITS OF STANDARDS	**EXPLANATION**
1.		
2.		
3.		
4.		
5.		
6.		
7.		
8.		
9.		
10.		

Now you know that the Joy of Standards comes from having standards in partnership with standardized work, it is time to understand when you need make this happen.

What problem are you trying to solve?

CHAPTER 2: WHAT IS LEAN?

Lean is a strategy

It can be argued that lean is a set of tools, a methodology, a way of thinking or even a strategy. For lean to be a sustainable continuous improvement approach it has to be strategic; this is the only long-term approach for your organization to sustainably adopt all the tools, methodologies and thinking.

If today your organization is not a lean enterprise, what will make it a lean enterprise? Tools will not change the thinking and methodologies will conflict with non-lean strategies. The only solution is: a lean enterprise is born from an enterprise which follows a lean strategy.

Put simply, lean is a strategy for your organization to create value and reduce waste for all stakeholders. Lean covers both sides of a metaphorical coin and generates significant cash for your organization when properly adopted.

Heads = Value, this is where you need to impress your customers. You need to have sufficient benefits and flexibility within your product or service.

Tails = Waste, this is where you cause yourself pain. You fail to efficiently use your resource towards the needs of the customer and consequently you do not operate as competitively as you could.

What problem are you trying to solve?

Heads: Create Value in the Eyes of the Customer

When you do not have enough benefit or flexibility within your product or service, standardized work can create spare capacity to deliver these without increasing the amount of resource required. Standardized work enables you to consider producing more variety, with smaller batches, with less leadtime and less effort for your customer. You can move towards a definition of "to standard and on time" that reflects the customer not your capability.

Example

Go to any Accident and Emergency department in Germany (outside office hours).

Complete the following journey;

a. Arrival administration
b. Triage by a nurse
c. Diagnosis by a doctor
d. Treatment by someone else
e. Confirmation by the original doctor
f. Departure administration

See that every employee is busy checking and walking. Then ask yourself, why were you served for a total of 20 minutes, but you had to pay 4 hours for parking?

This is a circumstance where an organization fails to deliver the value to a customer in the way that the customer needs. This missing value is the one that should be resolved when you want to create joy in the eyes of the customer.

What problem are you trying to solve?

TAILS: REMOVE WASTE TO BE RELIABLE

When you need more resource to complete the task, in the time the customer expects, you need to learn standardized work to reduce effort. This reduction enables you to complete the task with the resource you have and make your products and services deliver predictably.

EXAMPLE

Reflect on your last annual business planning cycle and ask yourself these questions:

a. Why did it take longer than last time to complete?
b. Why did people have to work late to meet the deadlines?
c. Why did it take more inputs from more people with more calculations?
d. Why did it need to start earlier than last year?
e. What logic drove people to change numbers until they looked acceptable?
f. Why did all that effort not translate into bigger results the following year?
g. Has it been forgotten why the annual business planning cycle was invented?

Within this example you can see unreliability being tackled with extra effort. You could also suggest that the purpose of the task has moved from "giving the business the knowledge to be confident with its plan" to "satisfying the requirement to do a plan". Efficient at not delivering the purpose has become the normal way of working.

There are circumstances where you need to remove waste to be more reliable and refocus your people on the original purpose of the task.

What problem are you trying to solve?

When following a lean enterprise strategy, both the **HEADS AND TAILS** scenarios are well tackled when using the Joy of Standards to solve problems and save effort.

However, you may be noting that this book does not recommend that you use lean for cost reduction. That is because lean is the wrong strategy to achieve this. If you use lean to reduce costs then you will attack your employees and customers for short term benefits. Outsource, offshore, downsize your people and your product's value, then customers will eventually go to your competitors. Think of it this way; if you shrink your costs faster than you shrink your sales, you will have more profit, but eventually you will have no customers.

There are 7 wastes that are tackled when tackling the tail of the metaphorical coin and 7 values which are enabled when tackling the head of the metaphorical coin. The next 2 sections of this book will explain these.

What problem are you trying to solve?

THE JOY OF STANDARDS / PAGE 33

7 Wastes in the process

As discussed earlier within this chapter, lean is a strategy for your organization to create value and reduce waste. Any solution which makes both of these improve for all stakeholders is successful.

There are 7 commonly recognized wastes within the lean community. These are shown within **DIAGRAM C** below.

DIAGRAM C: The 7 wastes tackled by lean thinking (and standards)

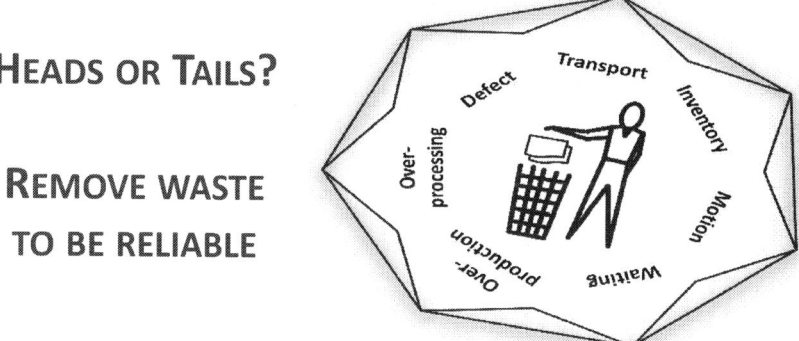

HEADS OR TAILS?

REMOVE WASTE TO BE RELIABLE

Many books explain and define these 7 wastes; I will quickly do the same. As your people become more familiar with standardized work, they will see these 7 wastes more and more often, even better, they will find ways to reduce them.

TRANSPORT is the waste you have when you move a product or service between locations and / or people in order to start the next step in the process.

What problem are you trying to solve?

People confuse transport waste with value in that they say "I moved it so we could add value" when they should be saying "it moved in one direction towards the ultimate customer, in all organizations, and never back and forth."

INVENTORY is the waste you have when you have products or components (including items necessary for a process) which are not going to be immediately used or sold. This inventory waste thinking conflicts with our economy of scale thinking; buy big and get a big discount. Inventory waste recognizes that you have to store, manage and move inventory and also that inventory gets damaged, expires or becomes obsolete; therefore always try to have lower and lower inventory. Inventory also allows for suppliers to hide poor quality, the lower the inventory the lower the number of defective components that you and the supplier will have to resolve when a defect is discovered. Consignment stock and customer managed inventory do not eliminate inventory; they just hide the ownership and / or decision making in ordering inventory. Lean recognizes all of these perspectives and always tries to lower the total inventory of both finished goods (at your organization and your customer's) and raw materials (at your organization and your supplier's).

I have a simple and completely unproven formula for the cost of inventory. It will lead you to think differently about getting bulk-buy discounts, it is as follows:

For every 10 days of inventory you, your suppliers and your customers hold, add 1% to the cost of your products; a new way to think about cost.

MOTION is the waste you have when an employee moves around their place of work in order to complete the process. This waste is best seen when you

What problem are you trying to solve?

stand in one place and observe people; I have seen people move over 3km in one day and they worked in an office. Do you pay your people to waste 2 hours walking every day? Save time, energy, injury and delays by eliminating unnecessary motion.

WAITING TIME is a waste the customer always experiences and your employees are very vocal about; someone is always waiting for someone else. Some waiting time is valued; if you are in an expensive restaurant you do not want your food in the same time as a fast food restaurant. Eliminate the waiting time customers do not value, like waiting for their check at the end of the meal or ensuring that when you say the fish will take 20 minutes they receive it in 19 minutes. They will be delighted by your organization's reliability (meeting your promises) and service (ensuring they receive hot, freshly cooked food when it is ready).

OVER-PRODUCTION is often called the mother of all wastes. This is because if you make more than is needed, you have inventory. When you have excessive inventory then two things commonly happen: you make customers wait as you search for the right product and you pay higher storage costs. Standardized work, in partnership with standards, is a great method to reduce over-production. When you have reliable and predictable processes, you can afford to make things either later than previously thought or when the customer asks. This is clear when it comes to a physical product and less clear for a service. Service over-production can be thought of as producing documents or information which are not needed for the process to achieve its goals (think reports which are produced but never read).

OVER-PROCESSING is when you touch, move, alter, enhance or check a product or service, more often than the customer truly values. Typing an address from one system onto a spreadsheet is a simple example, whereas

What problem are you trying to solve?

including features on a product that the customer does not value may be more difficult to quantify.

DEFECTS: if over-production is the mother of all wastes, then defects is the father. Defects create rework, write-offs and the need for inspection, they are prevalent everywhere in service based processes and over the next 50 years, hopefully they can be minimized in a way which has been similar to the achievements within manufacturing. Also be aware that a defect free product is not the same as a product the customer values.

ALTERNATIVE: Some lean literature will suggest unutilized talent as an eighth waste (or list 7+1 wastes). I disagree that unutilized talent is a waste for one simple reason: unutilized talent does not relate to the product or service; it relates to the people making the product or service. To maximize the use of talent I suggest fixing management with better ways in **MANAGING THE NEW STANDARD**, which are described towards the end of this book.

What problem are you trying to solve?

THE JOY OF STANDARDS / PAGE 37

7 Values for the customer

Lean literature discusses 7 wastes but rarely proposes a list of customer values. This omission is curious, is it because value is too hard to define or is it because the lean community is obsessed with waste and thinks value is just a consequence of having less waste than the competitor? I would like to propose a list, as value is something you should build into your process, during standardized work activities. This would ensure you deliver something which is valued by customers.

DIAGRAM D: The 7 values enhanced by lean thinking (and standards)

HEADS OR TAILS?

CREATE VALUE IN THE EYES OF THE CUSTOMER

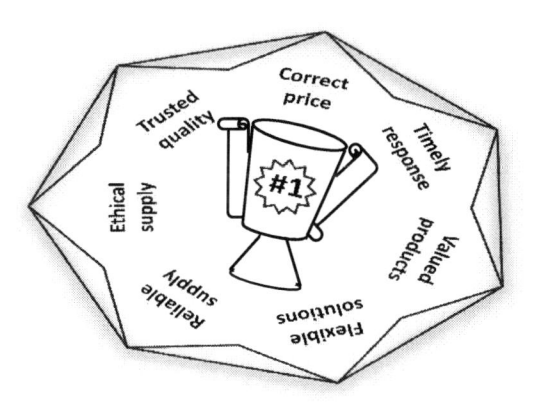

Trusted quality, Correct price, Timely response, Valued products, Flexible solutions, Reliable supply, Ethical supply — #1

These 7 values are not the opposite of the wastes. They are just part of the same metaphorical lean strategy coin. Like the 7 wastes they overlap and contribute to each other; there is no absolute separation.

What problem are you trying to solve?

This overlap happens when you deliver the right product at the right price with the right service with the minimum waste. You will need to use the Joy of Standards to minimize waste whilst you maximize value.

CORRECT PRICE is the first value defined as without the correct price you will not have customers. You can have the best product in the world, but, if it is too expensive then customers will select competitor's products and if it is too cheap then competitors will get higher margins and investors will abandon you.

TIMELY RESPONSE is also important and can determine what your customers are willing to pay. They will pay a premium or praise your organization (sometimes) for a fast service. Conversely customers do not always value a service which is too fast (or too slow) and conflicts with their expectations. The trick with timely response is to understand which response time will delight your customers. Empower your people, with standardized work, to make just-in-time reliably happen without stress, waste and defects.

VALUED PRODUCTS and services need to be provided. If your customers find features or aspects of your product or service which are consistently and obviously better than your competitors then they will choose you more often. Make sure you make these features clear and recognizable. The Microsoft Windows 7 computer (made by HP) I am typing on today has many differences to my wife's Macbook Pro (made by Apple) and the difference a potential consumer will value are the hardware, software, aesthetic and ergonomic features these computers contain (not just the $1,000 price differential that is charged in the local store).

What problem are you trying to solve?

If you believe that the market determines the prices, then lean agrees. Lean says profit is not cost plus margin, lean has a different equation for price; it is a counterintuitive calculation to guide an organization.

Profit = a fair price to the consumer less costs

Organizations should therefore use the Joy of Standards to increase value / reduce cost and increased profit will be the consequence. This is how lean organizations avoid the risk that their desired margin puts their product above the market price; they also avoid a shrinking market share as there is continuously more value within their products (at a price that market forces dictate).

FLEXIBLE SOLUTIONS are also a balancing act; too much or too little is a problem, like Goldilocks (in the fairytale) you will have to find something that is just right. This is because flexible solutions create complexity in your organization but can also create new or happier customers. You will have to choose the level of flexibility suitable for your organization. This selection will boil down to one double-barreled statement: how much growth will you get from this complexity and how will you remain competitive on costs and service when delivering this complexity? If your answers are not clear, then your flexibility decision should lead you away from tailored solutions until these answers do become clear.

These flexible solutions do not need to be restricted to a single proposition. Different market opportunities exist: Highly flexible, tailored solutions which you are in a unique position to provide, command a high market price. Inflexible, mass production solutions which competitors can make, command a low market price.

What problem are you trying to solve?

The trick with flexibility is to ensure you do not have the costs of the former when you are providing products of the latter. The trick with lean thinking and standardized work is to start offering the former with the costs of the latter and watch your profit margins and market share grow.

RELIABLE SUPPLY is a basic requirement of your customers, in 10 years of lean, I have seen this as the most commonly missed item of an organization when providing products and services to customers. Lean reduces inventory of finished goods and reduces work-in-progress within your office, distribution centers and manufacturing facilities, counterintuitively, this will actually make your supply more reliable. You will be able to predictably and reliably provide what your customers want.

Reliable supply is not limited to reducing inventory, it also relates to how your organization plans and sells its products and services. All three of the factors in **DIAGRAM E** interact and need to be optimized to ensure reliable supply.

DIAGRAM E: Factors which ensure reliable supply

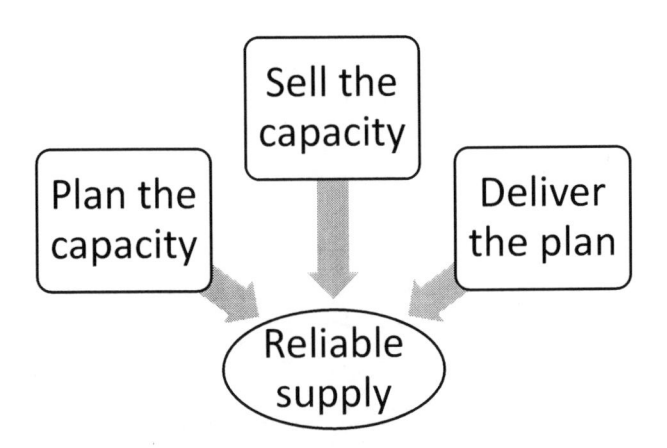

What problem are you trying to solve?

- Plan the capacity: how much can your organization reliably provide in the market place, find the number, communicate to sales and prepare to deliver that capacity.
- Sell the capacity: not a single item more or you will have an organization which is overstretched, any less and you will have an organization with excessive costs.
- Deliver the plan: have standards which will be constantly managed to continuously improve. See costs, quality and delivery that becomes more and more reliable.

ETHICAL SUPPLY is not just a new and trendy word. Ford doubled people's wages, Unilever built Port Sunlight and Tata is majority owned by charities. This corporate social responsibility is not new; it is part of ethical supply.

If your organization is leading in its industry, on the ethical perspectives that matter, then you will not experience the negative fallout from boycotting, strikes and social media attacks. It is a simple win-win situation in today's interconnected world. Promote optimization in your organization, through lean thinking, which makes you environmentally conscious, community orientated and accountable for your supply chain; your competitors will be green with envy, ruthlessly cost-cutting, cutting corners and left without customers or investors.

TRUSTED QUALITY is part of the DNA in all respected organizations. Your reputation for recalls, fraud and market manipulation is expensive to repair and inconsistent with your organization's articles of association. You must ensure that you not only sell and provide appropriately but you also sell and provide better than you did yesterday, only the Joy of Standards (with standardized work and continuously improving standards) can guarantee this.

What problem are you trying to solve?

The alternative to trusted quality is to stay stuck in the 1980s with a rule book to throw at suppliers and / or failing employees. This may save a few directorial nose bleeds, but over the long term it will not save your organization.

Now that you know about the 7 wastes and the 7 values, it is time to understand the definitions of standardization.

What problem are you trying to solve?

Some "standard" definitions to help

Many terms are used within the lean community, some of which you may already be familiar with. To assist you, and to complement any reading material you may already have, I have taken the liberty in paraphrasing some definitions below.

BEST PRACTICE / REFERENCE / GOOD EXAMPLE

A recommended, theoretical or one-off example, describing a process which may or may not be possible to follow. Written to guide people and share knowledge.

STANDARD / PROTOCOL / INSTRUCTION / SPECIFICATION

A definition of the process which is intended to be followed or a prescribed expectation of the result of a process (for example: the item should be between 2.0mm and 2.1mm). This document is based on requirements and / or observation.

STANDARD OPERATING PROCEDURE / STANDARDIZED WORK DIAGRAM

A visual and / or written explanation of the process; usually on one page with photographs and / or computer screen snapshots. Intended to help the employee when following a standard; in training and in practice. It should be referred to as the best known way of working.

STANDARDIZE WORK / STANDARDIZED WORK / STANDARD WORK

Different words for the same action. They all optimize a process by eliminating too much effort, usually to help an organization create value in the eyes of the customer and / or remove waste to be reliable, they discover better standards.

What problem are you trying to solve?

Last definition (I promise)

This is my definition of lean, given in a Polish car park one snowy morning, can you do better?

My definition:

> Lean is a way of thinking and doing to achieve your goals, with the customer in mind, and the minimum waste possible. Lean respects the needs of every stakeholder and ensures continuously improved sustainable benefit for all of them.

Your definition:

What problem are you trying to solve?

CHAPTER 3: FUNDAMENTALS TO LEARN

12 principles to guide you

Do you want to solve problems and save effort? These are within the book title for a reason; do not implement the Joy of Standards without the need for improving these. Standards and standardized work are a process which are taught differently, applied differently and managed differently. They are also a process which follows a common set of principles when effectively used, these are:

DIAGRAM F: 12 Principles to follow when solving problems and saving effort

Principles that **"PLAN"**	1st Empower a group of people
	2nd Establish a goal for improvement
Principles that **"DO"**	3rd Understand the ways of working
	4th Find a better sequence for the task
	5th Make the workplace easy
	6th Find a great way to follow the task
Principles that **"CHECK"**	7th Test the proposed way of working
	8th Evaluate the test
	9th Build consensus
Principles that **"ACT"**	10th Establish the new standard
	11th Train the new standard
	12th Manage the new standard

What problem are you trying to solve?

The sequence and overall categorization of these 12 principles needs to adapt according to your own organization and your own preference. The sequence described by me is roughly right, not precisely wrong.

Many people prefer to set the goal for improvement before understanding the current ways of working (to ensure that the proposal is not constrained by knowledge that a lot of improvement needs to be made). I happen to agree, however there may be situations where a lack of knowledge (of the process) is holding back the ability for the group of people to establish a goal; in these situations (or other situations like this), choose a sequence which swaps the **2ND & 3RD PRINCIPLES**.

Follow my sequence and categorization as a recommendation. The important thing is to not miss a principle because of omission. It is important to consider all the principles in roughly the order given or you will fail to achieve joy with standards: easy, reliable, repeatable and inexpensive processes that continuously improve.

Principles will be described in the chapters that follow, but what are these headings Plan-Do-Check-Act?

What problem are you trying to solve?

PDCA in one minute

Before I explain how your leadership will need to adapt to ensure successful application of the twelve principles, it is necessary to explain Plan-Do-Check-Act (PDCA). The PDCA cycle was invented by Shewhart in the 1930s and made famous by Deming in the 2nd half of the 20th century.

DIAGRAM G: PDCA cycle

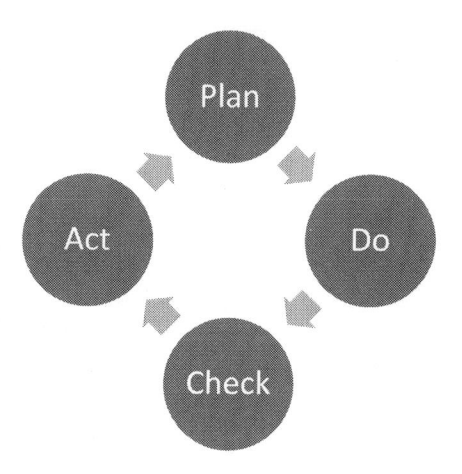

PDCA is a cycle to promote a step change improvement of a process and continuous improvement thereafter (the steep line on **DIAGRAM B** followed by the gradual improvement line).

Completion of one turn of the PDCA cycle leads to the beginning of the next; this is the essence of continuous improvement which comes from lean thinking.

What problem are you trying to solve?

The 12 principles I have described for the Joy of Standards are no different, they are just an example of PDCA. Each of the principles comfortably fits with one of the PDCA elements.

You should know that the PDCA cycle is often misused in 2 key areas:

1. **PRINCIPLE 2'S** "Plan" is often finished without the prediction and measurement of what success will look like. It often lacks a target or is not given subjective criteria. This results in the lack of understanding whether or not the "Do" will truly achieve the objectives that were originally required. This is often seen in projects or activities which are delayed or take a long time. Have you ever been in a project where the biggest issue is getting the team, half way through the project, to agree why they should be doing the project?

2. **PRINCIPLE 8'S** "Check" is often ignored or taken in a binary manner, by only concentrating on; was some work done? The PDCA cycle is more fundamental, "Check" needs to ask: was the improvement goal achieved? It also needs to study the effects of the "Do" and learn about what can be changed and therefore what can be improved, even if the physical aspects of "Plan" were carried out. It can be argued that "Check" is an opportunity to think about where the solution is applicable, this may well be the case, but "Plan" can also be the opportunity to understand this.

Do not fail either of these perspectives. Do not be someone over-eager to deliver results by concentrating on tools; remember what problem you are trying to solve.

What problem are you trying to solve?

Leadership success factors

Each of the twelve principles will be covered in the next four chapters. By the end of these four chapters, you will be able to implement the Joy of Standards. However, you need to discover some important success factors first.

1. Always do this for the benefit of the organization, the employees and the customers. If you only do this for one or two of these stakeholders, then you will not create a competitive advantage. Employees are not stupid, if you only do this to make them deliver more (or they may lose their jobs), then why should they adopt this new method to make profits higher? Managers are also not stupid, if you only implement for the benefit of the employee and customer, will your organization still be here in 1, 2 or 3 years' time? Lastly customers will not appreciate being optimized at their expense; they need to feel that your new standard for the task is better for them as well, or why do they rely on your organization to give them the product or service?

2. The role of a manager is not to manage the employee. Bucket loads of benefits from standards rely on a different skill set; the manager manages the deployment of resources to the correct part of the organization, the manager enables employees by removing barriers and encouraging them to improve the standard, the manager appreciates that the variety from the customer is the reason for variety in performance, the manager supports the standard with curiosity and continuous attention as to how it is helping their people. In summary, the manager's role is to be a leader and to coach a successful process. Leadership is not enforcing employees to comply.

What problem are you trying to solve?

Customer demand

Comparative text books, do put forward models for standardized work, these models usually include a reference to the following:

1. Understand the required outcome.
2. Understand the process.
3. Understand the takt time.
4. Rearrange the process to make it better.
5. Sustain the improvement.

The 12 principles described ensure this, except, I have avoided putting one particular aspect into them: the explicit use of the phrase takt time. Takt time is the regular beat at which you should produce your product or service. To calculate takt time take the available time in your organization to produce the product or service and divide it by the customer demand.

Takt time = available time / customer demand

EXAMPLE
When 80 parts are required today, and you have 7200 seconds of production time available (2 hours), then takt says that you need to make 1 part every 90 seconds.

This is beautiful and simple. You can manage your process with a new perspective, a perspective of flowing at the rate of customer demand. Every 90 seconds you can check if you are on track to meet all the customer demand.

What problem are you trying to solve?

Therefore you are able to act continuously throughout the 2 hours to fix issues; you do not need to wait until the end of the 2 hours to see if you have or have not met customer demand.

However, you will need to balance every step within the process to deliver within 90 seconds of effort and this requires a high level of process maturity.

WHEN IS THE RIGHT TIME TO USE TAKT TIME?
Ask yourself this question: Is every step in my process so reliable I am able to manage delivery, to within a few seconds, at every stage?

ANSWER: NO
Start by removing too much effort with the Joy of Standards. Help people who say their process is unreliable, unpredictable and in dire need of improvement. Any improvement will be welcome, the use of takt time is too far in the future to contemplate; a process that works more reliably than today is the requirement.

ANSWER: YES
Continue removing too much effort with the Joy of Standards and incorporate takt time. Incorporate the need to deliver at the rate of customer demand within the business goals as part of **PRINCIPLE 2: ESTABLISH A GOAL FOR IMPROVEMENT.**

What problem are you trying to solve?

Try before you buy

It is important that you can see the impact of standardized work on a process before you learn how to ensure this happens time after time in your organization. The best way to learn this is from an example. Place a pen and a piece of paper 5 meters away from yourself.

FOLLOWING THE 1ST PRINCIPLE: Empower a group of people.

Get a colleague to observe you performing the task on the next page. Take it in turns to perform this process. Only perform the shaded boxes when required. Perform the process at least 5 times to see the variation in the times when it is done. Use a continuous timing method and record in seconds (as shown in **DIAGRAM H** which follows: the difference between the time in each step is the time the step took). If you find that the process is difficult to time, at its various stages, interrupt the process, ask for the task to be repeated, but, find a way to find a roughly accurate time for the various steps.

Your results may be as follows:
- **ROUND #1 – TOTAL TIME 34S**
- **ROUND #2 – TOTAL TIME 38S**
- **ROUND #3 – TOTAL TIME 33S**
- **ROUND #4 – TOTAL TIME 57S (PAPER HAD TO BE FOUND)**
- **ROUND #5 – TOTAL TIME 31S**

What problem are you trying to solve?

THE JOY OF STANDARDS / PAGE 53

Pick up the pen game

DIAGRAM H: Pick up the pen observation template

STEP	COMPLETE WHEN	TIME IT TOOK TO PERFORM THIS STEP, OBSERVATION #					
		EXAMPLE	#1	#2	#3	#4	#5
1. PUSH CHAIR BACK	CLEAR OF TABLE	2S					
2. STAND UP	UPRIGHT	4S					
3. MOVE TO PEN AND PAPER	NEXT TO PEN AND PAPER	11S					
4. PICK UP PEN	HOLDING PEN	12S					
5. TAKE LID OFF PEN	READY TO USE PEN	14S					
6. DECIDE WHERE TO DRAW	HOVERING OVER BLANK AREA	15S					
7. FIND NEW PAPER	LOCATED NEW PAPER	N/A					
8. BRING TO TABLE	BACK AT TABLE	N/A					
9. DRAW LARGE CIRCLE	CIRCLE ON PAPER	17S					
10. WRITE NAME IN CIRCLE	NAME IN CIRCLE	20S					
11. PUT LID ON PEN	PEN LID ON	21S					
12. PUT PEN DOWN	PEN DOWN	23S					
13. MOVE BACK TO CHAIR	AT CHAIR	31S					
14. SIT DOWN	SEATED	32S					
15. PUSH YOURSELF BACK IN	IN ORIGINAL POSITION	34S					
16. SAY "NEXT PLEASE"	ANNOUNCED FINISHED	35S					

What problem are you trying to solve?

Do not change the process yet, you do not have the knowledge of what to change.

FOLLOWING THE 2ND PRINCIPLE: Establish a goal for improvement.

You now need to analyze the data that is already known; you can analyze your data or stick with mine. Remember, the purpose of this particular exercise (unlike real life) is to illustrate how you go about eliminating too much effort, not in finding a better way to draw circles (however much fun this might be).

For the mathematicians amongst you, calculate an average time that this task took, based on the observations made (you may use your times or my times, whatever suits you). This average is a guide to your elimination of too much effort, if it is wrong by a few seconds, does that matter if you make the right decisions and eliminate the waste?

The average time of Round #1, #2, #3, #5 is 34 seconds (34+38+33+31)/4.

The time of Round #4 was 57s, and is only needed once 3 circles have already been made, so it is needed in 1 out of 3 situations (remember the first observation did not have the "find new paper" it was magically already there – so that is why it is not 1 out of 4 situations that we have to "find new paper").

The average of the two types of observation are (34+34+57)/4 = 42 seconds (the rounding does not matter, the clock was not that accurate, so you are making decimal places on an approximate observation).

What problem are you trying to solve?

The process takes (from the observations undertaken) roughly 42 seconds. This is an important number, all improvement should be compared to this average; success will be evident when standardized work has eliminated effort from this number.

What will all the different stakeholders need you to do?
- The customer? The valuable circle and ability to know who did the circle (as they value the knowledge of who did the work, like an artist's signature).
- The organization? As many circles on paper as possible (efficient use of resources).
- The employee? The least effort possible, they have other tasks to do and they hate staying late to achieve them.

The goal could therefore be covering all these dimensions: Can you reduce the effort by 70%, find a way to draw more than 3 circles on one piece of paper and keep the customer's traceability.

FOLLOWING THE NEXT FOUR PRINCIPLES: You "Do" find a better process by:
- Understanding the ways of working (**3RD PRINCIPLE**)
- Finding a better sequence for the task (**4TH PRINCIPLE**)
- Making the workplace easy (**5TH PRINCIPLE**)
- Finding a great way to follow the task (**6TH PRINCIPLE**)

Due to the simplistic nature of this exercise, these principles have been combined into one analysis which will be used to demonstrate them all at once. The principles will be explained in more detail in **CHAPTER 5**.

A simple brainstorm of the process may produce the following ideas:

What problem are you trying to solve?

- Draw a line dividing the paper into 4 equal parts (this extra task will ensure you do not need to get paper after 3 circles, but hopefully the extra work will be offset by the saved searching time for new paper).
- Use a pencil, you won't have to take the pen lid on and off.
- Put the person next to the pencil and paper, no moving chair or getting up and walking around.
- Put the spare paper in the same work area as the person and their pencil (avoid the delay and effort of finding new paper).

FOLLOWING THE 7TH PRINCIPLE: Test the proposed way of working.

DIAGRAM I: Pick up the pen new process to test

STEP	COMPLETE WHEN	TIME IT TOOK TO PERFORM THIS STEP, OBSERVATION #					
		EXAMPLE	#1	#2	#3	#4	#5
1. PICK UP PENCIL	HOLDING PENCIL	1s					
2. SEE WHERE TO DRAW	MOVED TO BLANK AREA	3s					
3. GRAB NEW PAPER	NEW PAPER IN HAND	N/A					
4. DRAW LINES, DIVIDING PAPER INTO 4 AREAS	4 QUADRANTS ON PAPER	N/A					
5. DRAW LARGE CIRCLE	CIRCLE ON PAPER	6s					
6. WRITE INITIALS IN CIRCLE	INITIALS IN CIRCLE	9s					
7. PUT PENCIL DOWN	PENCIL DOWN	10s					
8. SAY "NEXT PLEASE"	ANNOUNCED FINISHED	11s					

What problem are you trying to solve?

Your new results may be as follows:

- **ROUND #1 – TOTAL TIME 16S (GRAB PAPER AND PUT 4 QUADRANTS)**
- **ROUND #2 – TOTAL TIME 10S**
- **ROUND #3 – TOTAL TIME 11S**
- **ROUND #4 – TOTAL TIME 11S**
- **ROUND #5 – TOTAL TIME 15S (GRAB PAPER AND PUT 4 QUADRANTS)**

It doesn't matter that this time you had two instances of the shaded tasks, it doesn't matter that you also had to draw quadrants, you should be saying to yourself, wow these times appear to be much quicker, maybe this is a winning answer. Maybe the customer, organization and employee requirements have been met all in one hit?

FOLLOWING THE 8TH PRINCIPLE: Evaluate the test.

Your new averages will be:
- No grabbing paper or drawing 4 quadrants (10+11+11)/3 = 11 seconds.
- With grabbing paper and drawing 4 quadrants (16+15)/2 = 16 seconds.
- With the mix expected the average will be (16+11+11+11)/4 = 12 seconds (old average was 42 seconds).

Least important question: Did you do what you planned to do (did you do the task and the trial)?

Most important question: Did you solve the problem (did the employee, customer and organization get what was desired by the goal set with the **2ND PRINCIPLE**)?

What problem are you trying to solve?

You have achieved your goals on all three fronts:
- This is an amazing 30 seconds (71%) quicker. No big investment was required; just a few simple changes which could release people for other more important tasks.
- You are using new paper every 4 circles not every 3 circles, saving the organization valuable resources.
- You have found a new "initials" solution to the "traceability" requirement from your customer, if they are happy with this, you have preserved the customer value and you have a winning solution.

When evaluation shows that you achieved your goals, the trials have worked, and the new optimized process should be implemented.

When evaluation shows that you have not achieved the goals, the trials have also worked and you should now go back to all the earlier principles and decide which ones need to change. You will need to repeat the trials until; they work, you decide that the goals are not worth achieving or the problem does not seem to be a problem anymore.

Your time and reputation are important so, in the unlikely event that you do abandon the activity, learn why you selected a problem you did not solve and make sure you minimize this selection error in the future.

Also learn (for the future) why it is now acceptable to not continue. Is it that there never was a problem or that the problem is just disappearing temporarily?

FINISH THE TASK WITH THE FINAL PRINCIPLES:
- Finish "Check" by building consensus **(9TH PRINCIPLE)**.
- Then "Act" by establishing the new standard **(10TH PRINCIPLE)**.

What problem are you trying to solve?

- Training the new standard (**11TH PRINCIPLE**).
- Managing the new standard (**12TH PRINCIPLE**).

I suggest, as the process is fairly simple and contains well defined boundaries, you use the timing sheet as the standard and instead of having the observation columns, give some guidance to people who are expected to do the task. The new standard would therefore be something like the following.

DIAGRAM J: Pick up the pen new standard

STEP	COMPLETE WHEN	TIME THIS MIGHT TAKE YOU	HOW THIS WOULD LOOK
1. PICK UP PENCIL	HOLDING PENCIL	1 SECOND	
2. SEE WHERE TO DRAW	MOVED TO BLANK AREA	2 SECONDS	
3. GRAB NEW PAPER	NEW PAPER IN HAND	1 SECOND	
4. DRAW LINES, DIVIDING PAPER INTO 4 AREAS	4 QUADRANTS ON PAPER	4 SECONDS	
5. DRAW LARGE CIRCLE	CIRCLE ON PAPER	3 SECONDS	
6. WRITE INITIALS IN CIRCLE	INITIALS IN CIRCLE	3 SECONDS	
7. PUT PENCIL DOWN	PENCIL DOWN	1 SECOND	
8. SAY "NEXT PLEASE"	ANNOUNCED FINISHED	1 SECOND	

Training would not be too complicated. It would only take a few minutes and would need to include rules on using the standard and managing the standard.

Without these rules there will be no continuous improvement of the standard and you will be stuck following **DIAGRAM A** (left on next page) and not **DIAGRAM B** (right on next page) for the rest of your life.

What problem are you trying to solve?

THE JOY OF STANDARDS / PAGE 60

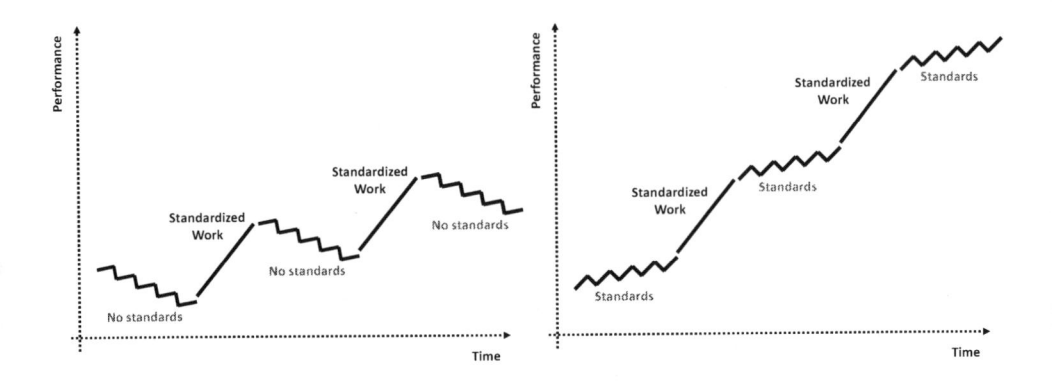

The points to note regarding this exercise start with the fact that I asked you to optimize the process, when it is my process. In real life, empowerment has to be to the people that do the work every day.

The next pertinent point is that each principle should be followed on a guidance basis, it matters that you think about the principle, not that you follow it blindly.

Each standardized work exercise that you participate in (or teach) will have a different set of circumstances, and no two situations will require the same investment of time and application of the principles. Some principles will be combined, some will happen in a different sequence and some may take a few seconds when the previous time you used them they took a few hours.

Implementing the Joy of Standards will release capacity in your people, if you fail to utilize this capacity, in a valuable way, they will find other things to do and your efforts are wasted. Hardly any benefit to the stakeholders will trickle through. In this exercise you released 71% of people's time. In accordance with the questions in the **2ND PRINCIPLE**, you must know how this can help your organization.

What problem are you trying to solve?

WARNING: Remember this is an experiment to find a solution to benefit all stakeholders, not a way to trick your people out of their jobs. Run your business for the long term and use everyone in your organization to help you make processes better; everyone can become more valuable than their cost.

The most important point to learn is the **8TH PRINCIPLE.** Was the goal achieved or not? People fall into the trap that some analysis was done, then some trials and then they forget to check that the solution actually creates the desired results. This is the hardest thing for people to remember to do; do not congratulate yourself for your efforts and forget about the purpose of the standardized work activity.

What problem are you trying to solve?

CHAPTER 4: "PLAN" WHAT TO DO

Empower a group of people

PRINCIPLE 1

Please allow me to take the position that people need to be empowered. Some of you may hold the view that you cannot empower people, but that you can only disempower people. If that is the case, I agree, as empowered people are the goal.

I have worked in an organization where a €3 under-payment by a customer has to be authorized by someone from a different department.

I have also worked in an organization where I was told to stop spending time trying to find an 8,000 dollar difference when multi-million dollar events were in the numbers, as my efforts would not change anything; other than the fact that I had an answer for the difference.

These situations, of disempowerment and empowerment (I leave you to decide which is which) are examples of management styles. In your organization, empowerment for standards and standardized work will need to be clear and unambiguous in their nature; how will you ask people to manage and optimize tasks? You will need to let people take decisions, without asking for permission, not any decision, but those which they are in a good position to make. Analyzing a real life situation, which I have seen in a medium sized business, is the best way for me to illustrate this empowerment.

What problem are you trying to solve?

Break paradigms not people

Communication at a 200 person organization was a mixture of constant noise and constant confusion; people would receive 100 emails about trivial matters each week and not hear about something significant that would impact their job. This could be called the era of the digital information overload.

The organization was also having constant complaint about this ineffective communication at almost every internal meeting. The biggest voices were the people that had been at the organization the longest and included well respected opinion makers who were outside the leadership team. These people did not respect the accepted way of suggestion; they would discuss informally at the coffee machine or publicly challenge leaders in town hall meetings. You might call them troublemakers, I call them opinion makers.

Empowerment of these people would be the opposite of what most organizations would normally do. The normal course of events would be to select a trusted professional to make a communication plan, require the opinion makers to respect this plan, and start communication solutions. For example; introduce a consolidation of everything important and communicate it once a month.

After several weeks of suggestion, the leadership agreed to a different approach. The opinion makers would be given the task of communicating in the organization, they would have full authority on how any subject would be communicated and would respect a modest budget within that responsibility.

This group of people now meet one hour a week and discuss what has been asked to be communicated, they brainstorm the best way to communicate that

What problem are you trying to solve?

and implement innovative solutions across multiple dimensions. They also acted on the feedback of constant noise and have implemented new guidance on how to communicate trivial matters; tell them and they will consolidate and send out every Monday morning. Never send it to the 200 people yourselves. The head of the organization was also asked to make this known to everyone and was also asked to follow this rule. If it is an urgent business matter that needs to be communicated, tell one of the communication team and they will find a "breaking news" solution.

The impact is staggering on multiple fronts. 100 emails to 200 people became one email plus a couple of business related communications each week to the 200 people. The main email is a newsletter with regular business messages / updates / events and social / charitable related matters summarized into a dozen segments – each with its own title and contact point for further information.

Also, the team now produces multi-channel communications for all key business updates and publishes just-in-time with innovative solutions, including a recognition scheme for people who have made a difference in the last quarter. The 100 dollar quarterly budget is sufficient for most needs; they ask when they need more. A testament to their success is that they have a waiting list to join their team.

This may sound trivial, but think about it, if every person in your organization is engaged in making things better and has responsibility for their actions, then every person is making a positive difference to your organization through empowerment.

What problem are you trying to solve?

You are not the expert

Choosing someone and giving them appropriate authority will not be enough. You will also need to choose the right range of people to help with standardized work.

If you are the manager, then like within the Preface to this book: "James, why do you tell your people what to do?" you are in a similar position. Empowerment is therefore not having a manager with a group of people doing what the manager thinks is best. Empowerment is asking a trusted group of employees to come up with a solution for a relevant business problem, letting them see if it works, checking with the manager if there is a business implication (like compliance and / or a customer impact) and getting it wrong from time to time.

SOMETHING TO TRY: As you will need to encourage people, try introducing a Giraffe award. Recognise the people who stick their necks out and do something that fails; everyone knows that people learn the most when they make mistakes.

Experts and high performers are a valuable resource in your company, do not ignore them, but do not let them monopolize the group of people that are going to optimize the task with standardized work. A balance is required of people "who know the answer" with people "who experience the problems". Your experts and high performers have techniques to help them, but they do not yet have a full understanding of how to ensure that everyone benefits from their knowledge, or why are they the experts and high performers?

What problem are you trying to solve?

By looking at the reasons why people may be a low performer or a high performer, you can minimize the risk of selecting the wrong people. Of course, with effective standards from **CHAPTER 1** being encouraged and ensured, the range should not be as extreme as shown in the diagram below.

DIAGRAM K: Proposed reasons for high or low performance

REASONS FOR HIGH PERFORMANCE	REASONS FOR LOW PERFORMANCE
1. Is well trained and has built a rhythm of consistent high delivery from their extensive experience	*The opposite?*
2. Selects the easiest requests	
3. Does not spend time helping others	
4. Does the minimum possible on a task	
5. Keeps knowledge to keep advantage	
6. Over-qualified for the task	
7. Leaves issues for other people to resolve	

A full range of people who perform the process will be a good selection for the team. Involvement of people who submit the requests for the process and receive the output of the process (if they are internal customers) should also be involved from time-to-time. This ensures that their perspectives are being introduced (and that their problems are being solved not being moved).

Try not to have too many people involved; too many people will result in wasting valuable time. Too few people will result in not enough perspectives being taken into account. The group of people you need is enough people to solve the problem.

Try groups of between 2 and 10 people and try to avoid more than this as this can start a committee which discusses problems and solves few. The size of the opportunity should dictate the amount of resource you dedicate to solving

What problem are you trying to solve?

the problem. A small problem only needs a couple of people for a couple of hours; a bigger opportunity can have more people for longer.

There is no right answer, the trick is to learn with experience and select a suitable group of people. In the meantime start with a few people, give them a relevant problem to solve (with a deadline) and see if they need more people to help them.

To define the goal, for the problem you want to solve, try following **PRINCIPLE 2: ESTABLISH A GOAL FOR IMPROVEMENT.**

What problem are you trying to solve?

Establish a goal for improvement

PRINCIPLE 2

The most important aspect for the standardized work exercise is to deliver a meaningful benefit to the stakeholders. As you are solving too much effort, the stakeholder you will impact most is the employee. You will release their potential for other duties.

WARNING: Do not release people from the organization, why would anyone help you manage and improve standards after you released people the last time you made an improvement? Find something better for people to do: growth, new products, quicker answers for customers or more improvement.

You also need to remember that the customer must never be compromised by your standardized work activities, you will need to determine; values to be preserved, values which can change and values which should be stopped.

I have worked in several European countries where the process involved the government, amazingly it is very simple to change how we worked with them; the only thing we had to do was ask, in a way, that kept the value of the process.

a. Can we have a quicker way of getting a document from one of your agencies? Answer: Sure use email instead of post.
b. Can we stop using a courier to your central administration headquarters and take it to a local office instead? Answer: No problem.

Solve the problem by changing the method; do not compromise the value that you get from the process.

What problem are you trying to solve?

The employee may be suffering from negative consequences of this process. These should be captured, so you can remember to eliminate them during your standardized work problem solving. These can include stress, boredom, confusion, overburden, variation in workload, unpaid overtime, a dangerous method or work environment and repetitive strain from a bad workplace.

Involving employees and empowering them will help them choose to solve the issues that matter to them. You may also be under an obligation to fix some of these problems, once discovered; do not forget to fulfill your legal requirements.

The organization may also have some problems with the process, maybe you are using more resources than required; perhaps the environment is suffering from excessive rework within the process (energy, waste, pollution, etc.).

All potential benefits (requirements) should be captured under the too much effort goal. This is the goal to give to the empowered team, no solution should be offered. If a potential solution idea already exists (and the exercise is to validate through standardized work that this is the right solution), then the owner of that idea should be consulted or be part of the team, empowerment is not people doing what you think should be done the way you think it should be done.

The next question to ask yourself is: how big should the goal be?

What problem are you trying to solve?

Why is seven(ty) the right challenge?

My rule is 70% reduction in effort. Sounds crazy, but think about it:
- Is 10% enough for people to see that the process has been improved?
- Is 20% enough for people to dedicate their time to this improvement?
- Is 90% realistic?

70% is a happy middle ground, more than half. It is a starting point, a line in the sand. Deliver 50% it won't be a problem, deliver 80% and people will be delighted, deliver 3% and you need to go back to the start. 70% works, it challenges, it finds new ideas, it does not accept the status quo and most importantly it gets people to rise to the challenge.

Putting a man on the moon in the next decade, was a challenge, you should be able to set a challenge for your problem that would benefit from standardized work.

If you are unable to set an appropriate challenge you are wasting peoples time, they could be doing something more useful instead, or they could just brainstorm modifications to the process until they get the required benefit, try the solution and update the standard (this works on goals which ask for a 10% improvement not a stretching 70% improvement).

I was once told that if I think of five ideas I am sticking with my current paradigms, if I think of seven ideas I am likely to discover something new. I believe that is why seven(ty) percent is the right level of effort elimination.

With this insight I was given an example; how many ways can I think of filling a glass? These were my answers:

What problem are you trying to solve?

1. With a tube, pipe or tap.
2. With a can or bottle.
3. By scooping out of a bucket or barrel.
4. By selling the liquid inside a ready to drink glass.

Now things get difficult, there must be some other ways, maybe a ridiculous way:

5. By freezing liquid into ice cubes, placing into the glass and melting.
6. By condensing vapor and dripping it into the glass.

Now things can only be solved by going outside of my paradigms:

7. www.youtube.com "Bottoms up beer dispenser".

Sorry but beer is only an example. I have no business interests or contact with the company that makes this beer dispenser – it was just a good example of thinking outside of the glass.

What problem are you trying to solve?

SMART goals

SMART goals (invented in the 1980s by George T. Doran) are a good guide to ensure that you are creating a goal which can be evaluated.

Specific: Which specific value / problem / waste requires a solution to be found; fix world hunger or help 100 farmers irrigate their fields?

Measurable: How will the group of empowered employees know if the improvement has been achieved if there is no value to evaluate their achievements?

Achievable: Empowerment comes with the responsibility to stretch but not to setup failure. The goal should be consistent with the actions that the empowered employees are able to achieve from a time, scope, technology, budget and authority perspective. Ultimately, achievability is from good sponsorship, good training and good support; leadership makes achievable happen.

Relevant: How will this action be useful to your organization, your customers and your employees? Investigation is not an action; an improved process is the requirement.

Time-Bound: When does this action need to be complete to ensure all the stakeholders are happy? 6 hours, 6 days or 6 weeks? Not 6 months or 6 years, this is standardized work, not invention of the next Amazon.

What problem are you trying to solve?

Summary of Principles that "Plan"

Application and success with the principles is not to be expected without thoroughly understanding what you are trying to achieve.

PRINCIPLE 1: EMPOWER A GROUP OF PEOPLE

You want to ensure that you empower people that can act on behalf of the team(s) that will accept the new process. Empowerment is about letting people improve their process, not about encouraging them to change other people's processes. If other people's processes need to change, you have empowered the wrong group of people.

Within "Pick up the pen game" you learnt that you need to involve the right colleagues for engagement and buy-in purposes. You also learnt that you need to share observation duties to get a representative view of how the process is done.

Chapter 4 teaches you that meaningful empowerment is required from both high performers and low performers. You should also consider involving "suppliers of" and "customers to" the process and ensure you choose the right sized team for the problem.

PRINCIPLE 2: ESTABLISH A GOAL FOR IMPROVEMENT

A goal which is inspiring is required, making it SMART brings clarity. Encourage people to stretch their ambitions, reward them for trying, do not penalize them for failing; do you want them to act or do you want them to wait?

What problem are you trying to solve?

Within "Pick up the pen game" you learnt that there are three stakeholders who are impacted when you change the process:
- Employees who want to keep their jobs and make them more meaningful.
- Customers who want their product or service with less issues / more value.
- Organizations who want their shareholder returns consistently higher.

Chapter 4 teaches you to think about what will be done with capacity released; as it is not to release people from their organization. This seven(ty) percent achievement, plus other benefits, will include many important opportunities. The trick is to decide what is important and not to be tempted to fix everything.

Collectively these principles need to establish a team of people who do the work, with a clear and meaningful goal on a process which they are empowered to act on. Any variation or sequence of these two Principles is a good variation if that generates this collective goal. Any adherence to the principles, which results in the collective goal not being achieved, was clearly not a good idea.

What problem are you trying to solve?

CHAPTER 5: "DO" IMPROVEMENT

Understand the ways of working

PRINCIPLE 3

Now that you have found a group of individuals who will represent the people doing the process, you need them to understand how the process is currently working.

First hold a meeting with the person or persons who recognized the need for the problem to be solved. Agree the goal that was established with **PRINCIPLE 2** as this then dictates which task or tasks you need to optimize.

Secondly decide which variants of the process should be included in the standardized work, is it every variety or just the common varieties. Within the "Pick up the pen game" you had two types of process variation; completion of the circle without the need to find a new piece of paper and completion of the circle with the need to find a new piece of paper. What is the mix within the problem you want to solve, how will you know you are seeing an appropriate mix / how will you know which weight to give the different items? All of these answers can only be done by studying the types of request within your task and observing the variation in what needs to be done.

What problem are you trying to solve?

THE JOY OF STANDARDS / PAGE 76

Observation, not a guessing game

Observe the process as it actually is. You may have a standard, process map, training document or best practice guide. These are good for comparison to the actual process, but they will not identify the issues and waste that your people are experiencing. Only observation will find the true variety of these problems.

IMPORTANT: Observation makes standardized work scientific not theoretical.

Let me illustrate with an example. Take off your watch. Place it out of your view.
Draw your watch and you will end up with a diagram similar to that on the left. Now draw your watch by looking at it and end up with a diagram similar to the picture on the right.

DIAGRAM L: A watch from memory (left) and from observation (right)

One observation is better than 10,000 memories. As a human being you filter reality, your memory is not accurate, you remember what you want to

What problem are you trying to solve?

remember and need to remember. You even change actual events to how you want to remember them.

With colleagues, I was once asked to watch a process for two weeks. It was a frequently done task by hundreds of people. Only with 187 observations would leadership accept that I had captured a suitable mix of observation. I suggest that you find a more pragmatic sample size above a few but below a few hundred, process trials with the **7TH PRINCIPLE** will tell you if your mix was good enough to work.

SIMPLE RULE: 10% of the time you expect to spend on the standardized work activity is a good place to start (observe for 2 hours if you want to spend around 20 hours optimizing with standardized work).

Imagine if you optimized a process without the knowledge that you had to go and get something; your proposed process would not be credible and would not work. No-one would accept that you had found a better process with standardized work.

Lean thinking follows this principle in almost every activity that it suggests. Go to the Gemba (the place where the work happens) and see what actually happens. A process has 3 possible versions; what you think it is, what it actually is and what it should be. Going to the Gemba is the only way to ensure reality replaces imagination.

What problem are you trying to solve?

Golden rules of Gemba

Written below are some simple things to do and follow whilst doing the observation at the Gemba (the place where the work happens). This list is not exhaustive but it helps and guides you towards success.

1. Respect people when they are being observed – they are experts – whatever they say is correct, observers do not need to give opinions, they are there to write other people's opinions and experiences down.
2. Try to share observation and being observed between the team members – consider changing the team if no-one actually does the process regularly.
3. Have a rotating chief observer, have them write down the observations onto paper (electronic recording usually results in the person being observed waiting for the observer to type) – write: what is done, who does it and how it is done. If the process is too fast, either ask for steps to be repeated or get permission to record the process (with a smart phone) and play it back later.
4. Consider assistance in the observation to record factual data and observed issues: how long did the process take to complete, had it been waiting, will it wait until the next step, was it completed, was there a problem, can a printout, photograph or screen shot be taken to assist memory when improving the process later?
5. Keep everyone informed, the people being observed, the team around them, what is being done and why it is being done – the wrong assumptions should not be allowed to exist – you do not want people to think that you are "optimizing them" when you are "optimizing the process".

What problem are you trying to solve?

THE JOY OF STANDARDS / PAGE 79

DIAGRAM M: Template for 5-10 minutes of observation

WHO & WHAT	HOW	DATA	OTHER OBSERVATIONS
MAKING A COFFEE EXAMPLE: CONSUMER USES A KETTLE TO MAKE HOT WATER (FOR A CUP OF COFFEE)	TAKE KETTLE TO TAP, OPEN LID, FILL WITH WATER, CLOSE LID, THEN RETURN KETTLE TO POWER SOCKET, PRESS ON BUTTON	6 TIMES A DAY 3s+1s+8s+1s+5s+1s OBSERVED FOR 2-3 CUPS OF HOT WATER EACH TIME	WALKED 2 METERS ACROSS THE KITCHEN. CANNOT SEE HOW MUCH WATER IS IN THE KETTLE.
1.			
2.			
3.			
4.			

What problem are you trying to solve?

Find a better sequence for the task

PRINCIPLE 4

You have an engaged team with a goal and an understood process from observation. You will need to solve several problems regarding the process to remove 70% of the effort from within it. You are solving too much effort within this book. If you want to solve poor quality, see the companion book **"PREVENT ERRORS AND AVOID DEFECTS: RETHINK QUALITY & MEASURES"**.

From an effort perspective, sequence problems fall into two categories: repeated work and waiting time.

Repetition and waiting time sounds basic, but when you were observing the process, how many people did the process pass between, did it pass forward and backwards between people, did the same activity get repeated or partly completed, only to be returned to later? Look at each step within your time observation, and see if any of this is applicable. Now evaluate the problem that happens on the applicable items, in other words, how does this impact effort?

Once this has been established, can you eliminate any of these problems by changing the sequence of the tasks? Would step 4 have less effort if it was done before step 6? Can step 3 be combined with step 8?

To discover how to make these sequence decisions, a typical airport scenario will be used as a guide for you to learn from.

What problem are you trying to solve?

THE JOY OF STANDARDS / PAGE 81

DIAGRAM N: A typical airport experience for any passenger wanting to fly

STEP	COMPLETE WHEN	TIME OBSERVED: SHARED TIME / CUSTOMER TIME	ANALYSIS
1.0 QUEUE AT CHECK-IN	AT COUNTER	100 SECONDS	
1.1 GREET CUSTOMER	HELLO EXCHANGED	10 SECONDS	
1.2 ASK FOR PASSPORT	PASSPORT HANDED OVER	10 SECONDS	
1.3 ASK CUSTOMER "WHERE TO?"	DESTINATION KNOWN	10 SECONDS	
1.4 START CHECK-IN	SEAT SELECTED	10 SECONDS	
1.5 ASK SECURITY QUESTIONS	CONFIRMATION RECEIVED	10 SECONDS	
1.6 ALLOCATE SEAT	SEAT SELECTED	10 SECONDS	
1.7 ISSUE BOARDING PASS	DOCUMENTS WITH PASSENGER	10 SECONDS	
2.0 WALK TO SECURITY	AT SECURITY	100 SECONDS	
2.1 GET BOARDING PASS CHECKED	BAR CODE SCANNER OPENS GATE	10 SECONDS	ALREADY ISSUED BY SOMEONE AT AIRPORT
2.2 WALK TO BORDER CONTROL	AT BORDER CONTROL	10 SECONDS	
2.3 QUEUE FOR BORDER CONTROL	AT DESK	100 SECONDS	ALREADY QUEUED BEFORE
2.4 ASK "WHERE ARE YOU GOING?"	DESTINATION SHARED	10 SECONDS	ALREADY ASKED BEFORE
2.5 COMPLETE PASSPORT CHECK	PASSPORT RETURNED	10 SECONDS	ALREADY CHECKED BEFORE
3.0 WALK TO SECURITY SCREENING	AT X-RAY MACHINE QUEUE	100 SECONDS	
3.1 QUEUE AT SECURITY SCREENING	AT X-RAY MACHINE	100 SECONDS	ALREADY QUEUED BEFORE
3.2 COMPLETE UNPACKING	TURN TOWARDS METAL DETECTOR	10 SECONDS	
3.3 QUEUE FOR METAL DETECTOR	SECURITY GUARD SAYS MOVE FORWARD	10 SECONDS	ALREADY QUEUED BEFORE
3.4 PASS THROUGH METAL DETECTOR	AT COLLECTION POINT FOR BELONGINGS	10 SECONDS	
3.5 COLLECT BELONGINGS	BELONGINGS IN HAND	10 SECONDS	
3.6 RE-PACK BAG	BAG RE-PACKED	100 SECONDS	
		120 SECONDS / 750 SECONDS	

What problem are you trying to solve?

By going through three hand-offs (three parts of the airport), it takes customers 750 seconds to complete the process (on a no variation scenario). Airport staff worked 120 seconds within that time.

Can you think of different ways to solve problems within the observed process?

a. How about the check-in clerk is the passport control person and by issuing the boarding pass, no-one else needs to check that the ticket is valid.
b. How short would the process be if steps were moved to the check-in desk?
c. If the process is broken down into different work elements, would a new (more logical) process become obvious?
d. How much airport space would that provide for shops, restaurants and airport lounges?
e. How much cheaper would it be to provide the airport services if the check-in clerk was the only person needed in the chain of people responsible?
f. Would there need to be queue marshals, or could they operate spare check-in desks and eliminate the possibility of a queue?

No question should be regarded as unreasonable. Statements regarding compliance, law and business rules should always be respectfully explored. This is where 70% ideas can come from. Do not be trapped in your paradigms, new competitors will not be trapped by them. In order to achieve joy with standards, you will need to eliminate, combine, rearrange and simplify the steps within your process until you have eliminated too much

What problem are you trying to solve?

effort. Failing to act on the process steps, with the right amount of challenge, will create an organization which is not capable of dealing with the future.

WARNING: Rules are not fixed, they are human inventions, make a decision on what should be done and then see how you can meet all legal and ethical obligations. Seek advice from people who can authorize a change in the rules and see what suggestions they can provide. If you encounter resistance, share the knowledge of the problem and ask them to explain the conditions which would result in an acceptable change.

Who says that a border control qualification cannot be attained by a check-in clerk, after all, border guards are human and computers / scanners can tell them whether or not the person is the person they say they are.

Who says that once checked-in, there is no opportunity to challenge people regarding their validity to fly, how about at the gate; where these checks often happen for UK & US destinations?

Could airports really eliminate so many steps just by adding step 2.5 to step 1.2? How much time would that save, would the effort be worth the reward? There is only one way to find out; build a proposed future process.

Rearranging for the better

I once found a new process sequence by using life size office layout templates in a car park. Paradigms are easy to break; a new airport layout should be no different.

What problem are you trying to solve?

THE JOY OF STANDARDS / PAGE 84

DIAGRAM O: A new layout for a new experience

STEP	COMPLETE WHEN	AV. TIME OBSERVED: SHARED / CUSTOMER	CHANGES PROPOSED
1.0 QUEUE AT CHECK-IN	AT COUNTER	100 SECONDS	
1.1 GREET CUSTOMER	HELLO EXCHANGED	10 SECONDS	
1.2 ASK FOR PASSPORT AND CHECK PASSPORT	PASSPORT CHECKED	20 SECONDS	CERTIFY CHECK-IN CLERKS FOR THIS TASK
1.3 ASK CUSTOMER "WHERE TO?"	DESTINATION KNOWN	10 SECONDS	
1.4 START CHECK-IN	FLIGHT SELECTED	10 SECONDS	
1.5 ASK SECURITY QUESTIONS	CONFIRMATION RECEIVED	10 SECONDS	
1.6 ALLOCATE SEAT	SEAT SELECTED	10 SECONDS	
1.7 ISSUE BOARDING PASS	DOCUMENTS WITH PASSENGER	10 SECONDS	
3.0 WALK TO SECURITY SCREENING	AT X-RAY MACHINE QUEUE	10 SECONDS	LOCATE NEXT TO CHECK-IN
3.1 QUEUE AT SECURITY SCREENING	AT X-RAY MACHINE	20 SECONDS	CUSTOMERS WILL ARRIVE EVERY 80 SECONDS ACCORDING TO STEPS 1.1-1.7
3.2 COMPLETE UNPACKING	TURN TOWARDS METAL DETECTOR	10 SECONDS	
3.3 QUEUE FOR METAL DETECTOR	SECURITY GUARD SAYS MOVE FORWARD	10 SECONDS	
3.4 PASS THROUGH METAL DETECTOR	AT COLLECTION POINT FOR BELONGINGS	10 SECONDS	
3.5 COLLECT BELONGINGS	BELONGINGS IN HAND	10 SECONDS	
3.6 REPACK BAG	BAG REPACKED	100 SECONDS	
		100 SECONDS / 350 SECONDS	
SAVING FROM LOOKING AT REPETITION AND WAITING TIME		20 SECONDS (16%) / 400 SECONDS (53%)	

What problem are you trying to solve?

As with any proposed solution, some assumptions exist. That is why there is a need to conduct process trials with **Principle 7: Test the proposed way of working**. Who says the queue at step 3.1 will be 20 seconds, will step 3.0 (the walk to security screening) be only 10 seconds? Will the check-in clerk take 20 seconds at step 1.2 or could it be less or more? How many clerks will be needed?

An assumption deliberately ignored was; are more security screening people and machines needed? My answer is "no". The current numbers serve customers today; a solution, that can use those existing resources, is all that is needed.

Security implications have not been considered within the proposal; will the airport security procedures, reporting lines and activities need to evolve to accommodate these changes? The answer will be "yes". The real question is; will the airport authorities be willing to try and find an answer which saves 16% of staff time and 53% of customer's time?

Making changes will not be easy, but they can be straightforward once everyone agrees that the changes are beneficial and all necessary requirements have been properly incorporated.

This airport scenario is just an exercise to start your thinking process; the real world will be equally complicated and difficult to change. However, you live in a world today where almost no airport operates with this thinking; they operate with different paradigms to those discussed in **Principle 4: Find a better sequence for the task.**

Warning: You are changing people's roles, what happens to the border guards? How will they be happy to make this change? A solution would need

What problem are you trying to solve?

to be found which satisfies everybody, implementing this solution without agreement and benefit to all stakeholders would make you one of the most unpopular people on the planet. Following **PRINCIPLES 7 TO 12** properly should prevent professional suicide, but you must do the right thing for all the stakeholders, the Joy of Standards must never be used to eliminate people. Do the right thing, not the wrong thing right.

What problem are you trying to solve?

Work Combination Charts

Too much effort has a source; it is from too little effort during a combination of process design (without standardized work) and process management (without utilizing standards). Simple effective solutions come from hard work and thorough investigation. The next example is an example of applying the right amount of investigation and thinking to solve a problem. It is a more advanced method for re-arranging, it uses a method called Work Combination Charts.

I was asked to assist a process which involved faxing orders to people at another location. We thought that our new faxed orders process was optimized, but it was taking 15 minutes in the trials, whereas our proposed standard wanted 8 minutes to be achieved.

Interviewing the people who had performed the trials, they told us the process was not working, as there were too many things to remember. They even told us that they were so frustrated with waiting for the fax machine, they even tried doing other activities during this waiting time, but this just resulted in them going backwards and forwards to the fax machine constantly checking if it had finished.

Their conclusion was that the new process was too stressful to go forward with. We said "just practice for a few days and see if it is a familiarity issue", they did and it still took 15 minutes to complete one order. The problem was not in the people or with their training, it was with the process; it was too complicated to complete in 8 minutes.

What problem are you trying to solve?

THE JOY OF STANDARDS / PAGE 88

We decided to use a Work Combination Chart to solve both the stress and the process time. The purpose of these charts is to show waiting times and repeated movements in order to prompt you into sequence suggestions which eliminate effort.

The chart works by displaying different types of activities with different symbols. All versions of this chart follow the same principle; what is the person doing within the process and what is the "machine" doing and how can activities be combined and rearranged to reduce effort for the person.

The first thing to do with a work combination chart is to observe the process and record the times each activity takes, a chart will typically look like below.

DIAGRAM P: Faxed orders Work Combination Chart (before **4TH PRINCIPLE**)

TIME IN MINUTES	1	2	3	4	5	6	7	8	9	10	11	12	13	14	15
ACTIVITY 1	■														
ACTIVITY 2		■													
ACTIVITY 3			■												
ACTIVITY 4				■											
ACTIVITY 5					■										
ACTIVITY 6						■									
ACTIVITY 7						▨	▨	▨							
ACTIVITY 8									■						
ACTIVITY 9										■					
ACTIVITY 10											■				
ACTIVITY 11												■			
ACTIVITY 12													■		
ACTIVITY 13														■	
ACTIVITY 14															■
ACTIVITY 15																■

On **DIAGRAM P**, activity time (doing tasks) is shown with a black shape. Waiting time is shown as a hatched shape (waiting for the fax machine to

What problem are you trying to solve?

send all the details to another office on the other side of the world). The person completing the process stares at the machine whilst it is faxing, no activity is shown whilst the waiting time is occurring as nothing is being done.

Now that we had visualized the process, we could then work on a solution. We asked ourselves; how could we design a better sequence to create less effort in the process?
- What should be done when waiting for the fax machine?
- Which activities can be eliminated, combined, rearranged or simplified to make the process take less time?

After several discussions, an unexpected idea came; you could call this the seven(th) idea. Why do we wait for the fax machine for one order? What if we took the previous order and left the current order on the fax machine? This simple answer would also fix the waiting time for the confirmation and the constant need to keep on checking the fax machine. It even had the advantage that a new faster fax machine did not need to be purchased. We would not buy our way out of the problem; we would solve our way out of the problem.

We had effectively decided that 1 item should always be in the process. This is called Standard Work in Progress (SWIP) – and is a common solution in standardized work to control variation and waiting times with a pre-defined level of Work-in-Progress between people or key activities within a process.

Following this idea, it was then easy to put the activities into a more logical sequence and remove most of the rework in going backwards and forwards between the activities. We had broken a paradigm, making the customer wait and rearranging the sequence would result in an ability to complete the tasks in 8 minutes not 15 minutes.

What problem are you trying to solve?

THE JOY OF STANDARDS / PAGE 90

A revised Work Combination Chart shows the new process with grey shaded boxes indicating the time when we are working on the previous order. Each cycle of the process would start one new order and finish the last (already started) order.

DIAGRAM Q: Faxed orders Work Combination Chart (after **4TH PRINCIPLE**)

TIME IN MINUTES	1	2	3	4	5	6	7	8
ACTIVITY 1	█							
ACTIVITY 2		█						
ACTIVITY 3			█					
ACTIVITY 4				█				
ACTIVITY 5 (LEAVE ON MACHINE)					█▒	▒	▒	▒
ACTIVITY 6 (PICK UP LAST ITEM)	▒	▒	▒	█				
ACTIVITY 7					█			
ACTIVITY 8						█		
ACTIVITY 9						█		
ACTIVITY 10							█	
ACTIVITY 11							█	
ACTIVITY 12								█

This is a paradigm breakthrough; the proof is with the fact that the overall productivity improves with a positive impact on the customer. It may take you a few minutes to take all this in, and to understand this better sequence. Therefore the next diagram should help.

Within **DIAGRAM R** you can quickly see that the new process has less effort and less waiting time for the customer (as the work is fully completed earlier every day). The SWIP holds the orders, ready for the next time an order is processed, so it only impacts time once (each new item into the SWIP does not add to the total time).

What problem are you trying to solve?

DIAGRAM R: Calculation of how long customers wait for faxed orders

>Order #8 arrives overnight
>7 orders arrived before it
>it is therefore 8th in the queue
>we start work at 9 am

>**Old way:**
>8 orders x 15 minutes
>= order #8 is finished at 11am
>the customer waited 2 hours

>**New way:**
>8 orders x 8 minutes + 8 minutes waiting time*
>= order #8 is finished at 10:12 am
>the customer waited 1 hour 12 minutes
>(including the extra 8 minutes waiting time)

*the SWIP only impacts the total time once

Lean normally says that waiting time is a waste; this is true. Aiming to make the customer wait longer than the minimum is not good business as this creates opportunities for problems by forgetting what the customer wanted. It also creates rework, chasing and complaints (see 7 Wastes in the process: **CHAPTER 2**).

The principle of making sure a customer does not wait is therefore a good principle, but sometimes a small amount of waste (SWIP) at the right point of a process can make a big difference to the total waste in your organization (too much effort) and the waste your customer experiences (total waiting time).

What problem are you trying to solve?

Now that you know how to find a better sequence for the task, even if it involves rearranging something as big as an airport or introducing Standard Work in Progress, with discoveries from a Work Combination Chart, you need to know how to make the workplace easy. If the task is in the right sequence and is difficult to perform, your people will revert to a different process, one that they find easy to perform, in other words your new process will not be a standard which is followed.

What problem are you trying to solve?

Make the workplace easy

Principle 5

Location, location, location is a common phrase in the UK. It means if you have the right location, you have a property which other people will value. The same applies to business processes. If all the components within the process and all the people involved with the task are located in a manner, which is optimum, you will have a process which employees, customers and your organization will value.

The main thing that can be reviewed when making the workplace easy is considering a concept called workplace organization. However, 5S (the workplace organization tool) is probably the most incorrectly used tool in the lean tool-box.

5S is a systematic way to optimize items at a work location so that people can find what they need quickly, efficiently and reliably. When things are not in place, or they are difficult to find, this hinders people from doing the task they wanted to complete in a time which should be possible. Every second counts in a business, your customers are waiting and even more importantly, they are paying for your service, if you make them wait, they will go elsewhere.

5S is five sequential steps to organize your workplace, all beginning with the letter S. It is well documented and widely used in the lean and six sigma communities, as with any widely used acronym or abbreviation, different communities give each letter a slightly different phrase and / or meaning. The important thing is to follow the process of each of the 5 steps, it is not important to have the same phrases.

What problem are you trying to solve?

Warning: 5S is often applied blindly as a program or a first experience, as it is easy to train and facilitate. Unless it is solving a problem of too much effort, every second you spend on 5S, is usually a second of effort that is wasted.

The 5S phrases that I use are:

1. Sort – decide which items are needed today or tomorrow and which items should go (permanently or to somewhere else) because they are either not needed or only might be needed in the future.
2. Straighten – decide the approximate layout of the new work area and where each item should be placed. Frequently used items should be close to hand and the overall flow of motion within the process should be smooth and one directional (think graceful arcs, circles and loops).
3. Shine – make sure that the new layout has every piece of equipment, apparatus, stationery item, cleaning item and essential signage in perfect working order. This is more than cleaning, this is inspection and testing. There is nothing more frustrating than starting a process to only find that something cannot be used.
4. Standardize – make sure that every piece of equipment, in the new layout, has a place which is clear to any person operating the process and that every time something is used or consumed there is a way to ensure it is replenished or reset.
5. Sustain – from shine and standardize, decide how the new process will be trained, maintained and inspected. The chance for reverting back to the old ways of working should be slim or none (and Slim needs to get out of town).

What problem are you trying to solve?

Spring cleaning for the right reason

I can give many stories where 5S has been used to make the workplace tidy, clean desks, organize stationery cupboards, even tidy kitchens and garages. None of these examples last. People revert to the old way of working. Spring Cleaning is not 5S; it is usually just the first 3 or 4 S's at best.

DIAGRAM S: Spring cleaning incorrectly with the 5S method

THE 5S METHOD	SPRING CLEANING
1ST SORT	GO THROUGH YOUR GARAGE AND THROW OUT EVERYTHING YOU DO NOT WANT OR NEED – WRESTLE WITH THE IDEA OF "IT COST A LOT OF MONEY"
2ND STRAIGHTEN	CREATE ZONES IN YOUR GARAGE AND RIGHT SIZE THEM FOR YOUR REQUIREMENTS – AN AREA FOR EACH IMPORTANT GROUP OF ITEMS
3RD SHINE	CLEAN AND REPAIR ALL ITEMS WITHIN YOUR GARAGE, CHECK EACH ITEM IS WITHIN DATE / IS WORKING PROPERLY – OR THROW IT OUT
4TH STANDARDIZE (SORT OF)	LABEL ITEMS OR SHELVING AREAS TO KEEP THEM UNDER SOME SORT OF CONTROL, CREATE STANDARD STORAGE UNITS WHERE POSSIBLE – USE THOSE JAM JARS
5TH SUSTAIN (FORGOTTEN)	COME BACK NEXT YEAR BECAUSE YOU DID NOT STANDARDIZE PROPERLY OR SUSTAIN THE IMPROVEMENT – AFTER ALL IT IS SPRING

Four things are missing from this approach. What is the problem, how much does it "cost", how focused will the implementation be and how will it be ensured that the problem never comes back?

First consider what problem was trying to be solved when fixing this disorganization? Is it that it takes 10 minutes to find everything to wash the car? Is it that every time someone wants to park the car, they have to move something out of the way? Or is it something more tangible like your children are starting a band and there is no way they are going to play loud music in the house.

What problem are you trying to solve?

Without a problem which ensures the first three principles are followed, why do this? Is a tidy garage just a quick piece of satisfaction which will dissipate after a few days?

Second, if you do not know how much impact the problem creates, how will anyone be able to justify keeping the new solution in place? If the problem costs 100 minutes a month and 100 Euros a year, it is known how much should be invested in implementing and sustaining the solution. If this is not known, then it is not worth putting 5S in place.

Think about all the improvement decisions you make in life; the ones that work are the ones where you know benefit (tangible or intangible) exceeds cost and effort.

Third, people need to let go of history when improving processes. 75 dollars was invested into a lamp which is no longer needed and therefore stored in the garage. Is it kept because it cost a lot of money or is it trashed because it is no longer needed? More often than not, things are kept in garages (and processes) because previous investment makes the decision to jettison the item difficult to make.

Paraphrasing a key principle in English contract law:

> "Past consideration does not form a contract"

Ignore the cost of the lamp (historical investment in processes); make a decision based on current and anticipated needs within the near future.

What problem are you trying to solve?

The lamp must go if it is not needed – sell it on eBay, give it to charity, recycle it – but do not keep it for nostalgia.

Last, how will it be ensured that the next lamp does not happen? Good standards will determine what should be done when the next lamp is considered for the garage.

Great sustainment processes will ensure that the standard and compliance to the standard is consistently and periodically reviewed and inspected. Sounds like wasted effort? Not if you think about the effort that is avoided by a repeated spring cleaning when the standard was not effective.

What problem are you trying to solve?

Stationery not stationary

Faced with a problem; you cannot find stationery in your office. So what? It costs a few people a few moments to find something. We had the same problem, however, it did not cost that to the people that were near the stationery cupboards, it cost them hours of disturbance every day. There was not a lack of standards (ask if you cannot find) but there was too much effort in ensuring the standards were followed (answer the question when asked). We set the goal that we would eliminate this disturbance time and release the time for other activities.

We conducted a 5S activity on the envelope cupboard as it was used by 180 people. It took one afternoon to resolve: my guidance and two of the people that sat next to the stationery cupboard.

We then implemented the first 3 steps of 5S with no real fuss. We found a lot of electronic equipment that was incomplete and no longer used – straight to recycling, it didn't matter that it cost hundreds of dollars – it was junk.

We implemented a new standard (the 4th step of 5S):
- Every envelope would be stored in its own section, with a clear label and description (no problems would happen when someone looked inside).

- A photograph of each envelope would be placed on the outside of the cupboard so that anyone looking would know instantly where to go inside the stationery cupboard (no need to ask where something is).

- Each section would have its own re-ordering card wrapped around some of the envelopes with an elastic band – get to a low level of envelopes,

What problem are you trying to solve?

place the re-ordering card in a tray (no need for an administrator to do a weekly stock check).

DIAGRAM T: Stationery cupboard living up to its new standard

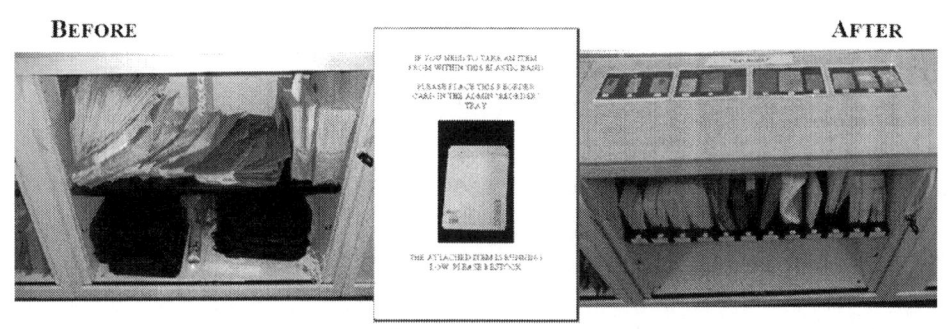

BEFORE   **AFTER**

RE-ORDER CARD

In accordance with the 5th step of 5S, two things were introduced to sustain the solution. We did not want to slip back into the old ways of working and fill the space we had released with junk and reintroduce the disturbances that came with chaos:

- Every week someone would use the re-order cards to order new envelopes.

- Whoever puts the stationery back in the cupboard (after a stationery delivery) will spend a few moments checking that the standard is working.

We ensured, in one afternoon of 5S activity, that the standard was always effective; it would not need modifying because something changes or someone stops doing it properly, the process would tell us if a problem occurs. We had a solution which we believed was self-sustaining.

What problem are you trying to solve?

So what? We released 50% of the cupboard space. We used less stationery in the next few months as we used up some excessive stock. We could always find the stationery so we saved a few moments. Not impressive – break even at best. The real test is what happened afterwards.

The team that sat next to the stationery cupboards repeated the exercise for the rest of the cupboards. Two months later I happened to visit them, the solution was still in place, with a standard that was slightly improved (order numbers on the order cards) and was still working.

So what? The people that sat next to the stationery cupboard saved so much time, that one person now spends every afternoon doing a different (important) task –something that enhances their career path; definitely a benefit worth the exercise.

These are the two true values of 5S which you should remember:

Faster solutions for customers as people are not wasting time trying to find things or set things up; they are delivering the process the customer needs.

PLUS

Time saved when using the equipment or workplace (and what can be done with that time saved).

What problem are you trying to solve?

Find a great way to follow the task

PRINCIPLE 6

Whilst finding a better sequence for the task (**4TH PRINCIPLE**) and establishing an organized workplace (**5TH PRINCIPLE**) it is also important to consider how the visual clues within the process aid and guide people (**6TH PRINCIPLE**).

How could **DIAGRAM Q** (Faxed orders Work Combination Chart) be easy to follow?

TIME IN MINUTES	1	2	3	4	5	6	7	8	9	10	11	12	13	14	15
ACTIVITY 1	■														
ACTIVITY 2		■													
ACTIVITY 3			■												
ACTIVITY 4				■											
ACTIVITY 5					■										
ACTIVITY 6						■									
ACTIVITY 7							▨	▨							
ACTIVITY 8									■						
ACTIVITY 9										■					
ACTIVITY 10											■				
ACTIVITY 11												■			
ACTIVITY 12													■		
ACTIVITY 13														■	
ACTIVITY 14															■
ACTIVITY 15															■

As photography with smart phones and color printing are so readily available, this is now an easy question:

i. Put the steps that are required to be followed, and show their sequence on a photograph.

ii. Use the visualization of the process as an opportunity to make the location of the activities take less effort.

What problem are you trying to solve?

THE JOY OF STANDARDS / PAGE 102

If every step is harmoniously placed with the equipment and adjacent activities, then the process will be easy to follow, reinforcing the proposed solution; make it easy for the employee to follow the standard.

DIAGRAM U: Faxed orders with a visual solution

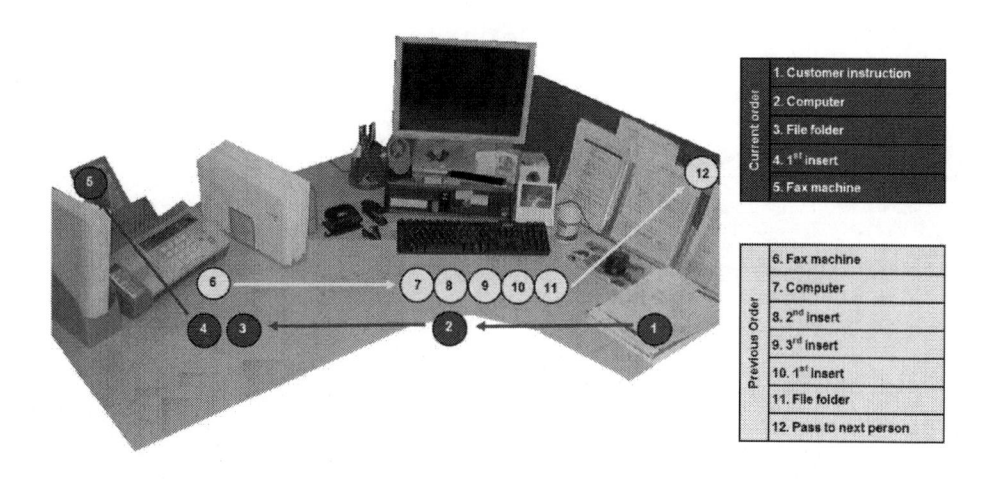

Current order	
1. Customer instruction	
2. Computer	
3. File folder	
4. 1st insert	
5. Fax machine	

Previous Order	
6. Fax machine	
7. Computer	
8. 2nd insert	
9. 3rd insert	
10. 1st insert	
11. File folder	
12. Pass to next person	

See how the process flows from left to right bringing the person who completes the process to the right place at the right time. The color code also distinguishes the current order and the previous order. The 3rd & 4th activity leave the items next to the fax machine ready for when the 5th activity is finished. The 7th-11th activity are all performed together in the same location (as the computer is needed). The 12th activity takes you to then next order (the 1st activity) to ensure a continuous flow of the process, even when these activities move to the next customer request.

Notice how the photograph is a real desk with various items, personal and business; no workplace organization was required. The process and these

What problem are you trying to solve?

items did not have a conflict from being unorganized or messy, so why would using 5S make the process better?

Visual management is a vital part of finding an easy way to follow the process. The solution you should implement should be as easy as ordering a Swedish chicken salad. The photograph of the new sequence for faxed orders is highly visual, and when placed in the workplace, ensures that there is constant reminder of the easier way to use the standard (for the employee completing the process).

When finding your solution remember that different people, who will follow the process, have different requirements. 1 in 10 men are color blind, I have even worked with a colleague that could not cope with the screen resolution due to poor eyesight, so we chose to printout each item and manually review it (the team thought that as it was only one person there should be an exception, I persuaded them to make everyone do this and use this sub-optimization as a reason to inspire continuous improvement when using the new standard).

Visual solutions do not just have to show you the process that is being followed; they can also show you what is acceptable and unacceptable within a process. My smartphone volume control shows me red when I select a volume which is likely to damage my ears, my car makes an audible and visual warning when petrol is low and the road signs I follow are designed with visual management in mind.

These are visual management solutions to guide you through various processes. Find the best visual management solutions for your process and see how people become successful in negotiating processes better.

What problem are you trying to solve?

Summary of Principles that "Do"

Within the principles that "Do" you will find a potential solution which will eliminate effort for your people whilst preserving or enhancing the product or service that is delivered. From good observation with **PRINCIPLE 3** and a pragmatic combination of **PRINCIPLES 4, 5 & 6** you will find the optimum solution. Not every problem needs every principle to be followed in full.

PRINCIPLE 3: UNDERSTAND THE WAYS OF WORKING
You want to ensure that, through observation, you know how the process is completed to make informed decisions about how to make it better. Within "Pick up the pen game" you learnt that watching the process as it is performed, at the place where the process happens, is the best way to observe even if you have to follow people as they move. It is also necessary to time the current effort levels, being roughly right, not precisely wrong.

Chapter 5 teaches you that you need to define which tasks need to be observed to find a meaningful mix of activity normally done. Only observation will suffice, through the watch game you learnt that memory is not as good as observation and multiple observations will probably be necessary.

PRINCIPLE 4: FIND A BETTER SEQUENCE FOR THE TASK
You want to ensure that you think about which steps should follow each other and how this can minimize the amount of work required. This sequence should not be restricted by paradigms which already exist, any sequence should be considered.

What problem are you trying to solve?

Within "Pick up the pen game" you learnt how to use apparatus more quickly (by using a pencil you avoided having to deal with a pen lid). You also learnt to eliminate the need to move around the workplace to complete the process (putting the person next to the pencil and paper to avoid movement).

Chapter 5 teaches you to create a view of the process which shows time elapsing within a Work Combination Chart. You can then eliminate waiting time (or find something else to do during its occurrence) and reduce the number of times a particular step needs to be revisited.

Principle 5: Make the workplace easy

You want to ensure that you use a layout which will guarantee the process will be completed correctly and consistently. Within "Pick up the pen game" you learnt to put the spare paper in the same work area as the pencil and paper to avoid unnecessary effort when completing a process.

Chapter 5 teaches you to find solutions which will be easy to follow and easy to sustain. The 5S tool showed you how to create significant results when followed properly; creating and sustaining the new layout to realize a worthwhile benefit.

Principle 6: Find a great way to follow the task

You want to ensure that the keenest sense (sight) is used to guide your colleagues to successfully complete the process. Different colleagues will have different ideas on how this should be; you need to find the optimum that guides everyone consistently; continuous improvement is not always having the perfect solution.

Within "Pick up the pen game" you learnt that processes are confusing; a solution that ensures everyone is successful needs to be found. Drawing a line

What problem are you trying to solve?

on the paper to divide it into 4 sections ready for the circle was a visual way to ensure the circles are in the right place and that people use the right amount of space, no matter who is completing the process.

Chapter 5 teaches you that visual solutions are solutions which ensure guaranteed success with the new sequence / layout and use anything to help the employee succeed. Push or pull on a door, visual solutions will tell you the answer; avoid hiding behind rules to keep the door aesthetically pleasing but difficult to use.

Simplicity has to become part of the solution. Breaking paradigms to find the best process (even if it is not logical) will be the answer which will reduce too much effort.

WARNING: What problem are you trying to solve? All of this activity is to meet the requirements established in **PRINCIPLES 1 AND 2**. Do not be a tool head and use these solutions without a problem to solve.

What problem are you trying to solve?

CHAPTER 6: "CHECK" ACHIEVEMENT

Test the proposed way of working

PRINCIPLE 7

Following on from the **3RD, 4TH, 5TH AND 6TH PRINCIPLES** you have a solution which you believe will work. Now you need to give your organization evidence that the solution does work or discover that the solution needs to be modified. The world's best forecast is a forecast and as such is just an educated guess. The same applies to your proposed solution. Until you have tested it, you are assuming that your solution is the current best way to complete the process. Just remember, assume is an easy way of making an ASS out of U and ME

Within your empowered group, try the solution for at least double the time of the observations you completed in **PRINCIPLE 3**. Why double? To prove to people (that doubt you) that you are being thorough. To prove to yourselves your solution is not a fluke. To ensure no common scenarios were missed in your initial observation, as all common scenarios need to be robustly handled by the solution.

Where and when you should conduct trials is an important consideration. If the process is busy at a certain time, then it is important to conduct trials at these times. Is it Monday mornings, is it 3pm every day, is it the last week of the month or even the last month of the year? Your trials must consider the variety of demand to the extent that you are able to test.

Trials do not always work, sometimes you will need to start them again. Perhaps the process was interrupted to conduct your trials or your solution

What problem are you trying to solve?

overlooked an important fact and needs to be reworked; this is why you are conducting trials.

Now find some volunteers from outside your empowered group (and anticipate the **9TH PRINCIPLE** of building consensus). Overcome some bias you and your colleagues may have, at least to the extent that gives your organization confidence.

DIAGRAM V: Building confidence with trials within your process

Scenario	Initial Observation	1st set of trials	2nd set of trials
A			
B			
C	Scenarios covered by solution		
D			
E			
F			

Examples of these scenarios could be:
a. Options on items you are manufacturing.
b. Different types of customers.
c. Simple and complex orders.
d. Different ways of communicating (post, email, telephone, face to face, etc.).

What problem are you trying to solve?

You agreed with your leaders that the old process was inadequate for the combined needs of your organization, employees and customers. This new process is being proven as adequate for most scenarios; therefore it is better and should be implemented.

If Kennedy had waited for the absolutely perfect solution for putting a "man on the moon and returning him safely", we would still be waiting for it to happen. This focus on the problem to be solved, with the best answer found, ensures that PDCA is not Please-Don't-Change-Anything.

What problem are you trying to solve?

Evaluate the test

Principle 8

You need to check if the predictions and requirements set in **Principle 2** have been achieved. If they have been almost met or exceeded, then great you have yourselves a solution you want to implement. If they have been missed, then great you have yourselves an opportunity to find a better solution (and you avoided implementing a bad solution).

Check will need to be multi-dimensional. It is a judgment call over several factors:

1. Did you understand enough scenarios to be confident with the solution?
   Yes – you are confident that the trials used enough scenarios – feed this knowledge into the future standard as the expected scenarios to be used by this process.
   No – go back to trials until you are able to say yes.

2. Did you have acceptable variation in process performance?
   Yes – the variety of performance seen is within the limits colleagues regard as acceptable – feed this into the standard as the expected time.
   No – to start with there was variation in performance, with experience this got better – feed this into training requirements and visual solutions when rolling out the new process – or this variation in performance will exist when other people adopt the process.
   No – the quality or effort was variable and gives your team concern – identify the problem, find a solution and restart trials until you are able to say yes.

What problem are you trying to solve?

BRIEF STATISTICS LESSON: Acceptable variation in a process is where you say that the process performance is within an upper limit and a lower limit which you find acceptable most of the time. Most of the time is usually taken as 95% of the time for decision making purposes; you may have a situation where your process needs a higher percentage. The upper and lower limits are defined by the stakeholders and will usually consider several measures.

Example: to know how many customers your supermarket can handle, with an optimized checkout process, you will want to know the following: range of total customer times at the checkout (including queuing time and serving time), the range of time it takes to serve customers (number of staff required) and you will want to define a very high accuracy for calculating the total bill / change due to the customer (avoid corporate losses).

3. Do the people who completed the trials agree that the standard was an answer that can be followed and should be implemented?
   Yes – get them to support you in consensus building.
   No – address every concern possible until they are happy.

You have to recognize that checking the right thing is not something that comes naturally. Everyone checks, but there is tendency to check what was last remembered to be done. In which case, you will likely check; were trials conducted? Did they complete? If the answer is yes, then people usually conclude that the solution should be implemented.

Please do not fall into this trap; please remember the purpose of the improvement. The correct question is one which confirms that the process:
- Is better for the employee, customer and organization.
- Takes less effort and people say it is easier to complete than previously.
- Delivers the product to the customer faster and with fewer problems.

What problem are you trying to solve?

Let me illustrate with a classic phone call to almost any service provider. Customer service measures are often orientated around: was the call answered within three rings? Was the call closed within three minutes? Answer yes and go home happy.

Now look at the reason for the customer call, and ask a different question. Was the customer problem fully answered without any difficulty to the customer? Answer no and see that bad service was given. The last question is seldom asked; this is what should be checked.

What problem are you trying to solve?

Checking your fax

Earlier in this book, I described an example of faxed orders. I described the situation where we had an original process, made an improvement (1st solution) and saw that it was not acceptable. We followed the **4TH PRINCIPLE** to improve the process (2nd solution).

DIAGRAM W: Faxed orders: Evaluation of improvement

	Starting position	Goal given	1st solution	2nd solution
Effort in process	15 mins	8 mins	15 mins	8 mins
Customer view	Next week	Within 24 hours	Within 24 hours	Within a few hours
			Check = need less effort	Check = great result, implement

Notice how in this example the customer view is that it originally took a week to complete a faxed order. We achieved the goal set for the customer with the first solution, but we did not achieve the goal set for the employee / organization. In fact, if you remember correctly the employees said they were stressed and confused so we had a situation opposite to what the employees wanted.

What problem are you trying to solve?

This was a great example of check; all stakeholders have to benefit and that includes the employees. The revised solution was built by the employees that experienced the increased stress and confusion, once they were happy, everyone else would be happy.

Their colleagues trusted and respected their judgment (as they had spoken when a change was not beneficial) and therefore the door is open to accept the new way of working, but this should not be taken for granted.

Even when the proposed way of working is tested and this new way of working is proven to your team (that the goals have been met), you still need to get everyone to agree, you need to build consensus.

What problem are you trying to solve?

Build consensus

PRINCIPLE 9

You have a solution, which has evidence that it addresses the problem. You now have to put yourself in the shoes of everybody else. They do not know your solution is better than today, they do not know it is worth accepting and adopting or they might not even agree that there is a problem. You need to buy-in various stakeholders.

The best way to create buy-in is to include people from the start, did you think about including someone from your stakeholders within your empowered group? Sometimes, in order to change a process, you need to include people from compliance, quality or the local union / works council.

However you are at **PRINCIPLE 9** not **PRINCIPLE 1** and you can never include everyone in the empowered group; so you will have to do something. Whenever bringing someone to your solution, start with the problem. Get them to agree to the problem, get them to agree that it needs to be resolved. Then show how you analyzed and resolved issues until a solution was found, tested and proven as effective. Their buy-in will grow as you answer their questions.

Two paradigm shifting solutions that I have seen will illustrate this.

What problem are you trying to solve?

Employee scores not robot wars

A manufacturing process was taking 60 seconds to complete. The process was: robot picks up plastic molded product, takes to employee, puts the object down, and returns to the molder. Meanwhile the employee made the part ready for the next process step. All of this was taking 60 seconds and employee feedback was that the whole process was rushed. The robot arm was speeding towards them and made them panic. The solution implemented followed **PRINCIPLE 6** and found an easy way to follow the process. The robot arm speed was reduced to be as slow as possible when going towards the employee. It did not move quickly to the employee and quickly back, to wait 40 seconds. It moved slowly to the employee and quickly back to wait 0 seconds (before picking up the next part).

As part of buy-in some union members were asked to try the new process. We asked one question, how long did the new process take? They said now that the arm was moving slowly the process was taking more than 1 minute and was acceptable as a change to the workplace. We then revealed that it was taking 50 seconds, we had removed the feeling of being rushed as there was no need to panic and check to see if a speeding robot was about to drop more work onto you.

It all sounds so simple? Well, why did we not have the 50 second solution in the first place? Why did the union need to check and approve our solution? The answer is: standardized work discovers solutions that are easier and more relevant because it does not take an easy path. Standardized work takes a focused and effective path to finding the simplest workable solution for everyone involved.

What problem are you trying to solve?

Red tape disintegrates

An information process (registering an employee with the government for unemployment insurance) was taking 2 weeks to complete (including data entry by our offshore provider). For the last few years, forms were sent by recorded delivery to the government, who would then issue a number and send back the original documents. One of the employees suggested we phone the government, get the number and send the documents by email with the number as the email reference.

As coach to the group, I was a bit unsure – would a government department agree to such a radical change? Of course, I should have trusted the empowered group; they knew the people in the government department would prefer this solution. A couple of meetings later and it was all agreed. Unbelievable, the government would change, it processed the documents in 1 hour not 2 weeks, saved everybody effort (and the cost of a courier to make the delivery).

The solution kept growing with **PRINCIPLES 8 AND 9**, why did we send the number to an offshore provider to be put onto our IT system? The answer: we had a contract for all data entry by this offshore provider. The reality was bizarre: we were spending more time facilitating the offshore provider's entry than it would take for us to enter it ourselves. We now enter the number on the IT system immediately after the phone call with the government. We even carried on paying the offshore provider for the service (until the next contract renewal discussion came up); after all, it was less effort for us to do the work than to carry on asking the offshore provider to do it.

What problem are you trying to solve?

Summary of Principles that "Check"

Check is not a tick in a box. It is a can of worms. Make sure that there is honest and open discussion on whether or not the solution is better for everyone; build consensus and remember this is not the same as "I do whatever I want" consultation. If you never have these discussions and never go back to find better solutions, you are not performing check; you are "just do it, I know better".

PRINCIPLE 7: TEST THE PROPOSED WAY OF WORKING
You want to ensure that the proposed solution will work in a realistic way. Within "Pick up the pen game" you learnt to conduct trials with a test, in as real an environment as possible*, so you know that the new solution is undeniably better in all stakeholder dimensions.

*live testing should always be limited to how much your organization will be impacted by a failure; internal processes do not have the same reputational problems as processes which impact external customers. Be mindful when conducting trials, do not expose employees and organizations to unacceptable risk.

Chapter 6 teaches you to select the right time and the right people to test the process. Starting with your empowered team, and expanding to other people that will be asked to adopt the new process, ensures that acceptance of the new solution is easier. Chapter 6 also told you to ensure you cover the scenarios you already expect and to consider spending longer on trials (roughly double the time) than you did on observation in **PRINCIPLE 3: UNDERSTAND THE WAYS OF WORKING.**

What problem are you trying to solve?

Principle 8: Evaluate the test

You want to ensure that the solution meets the requirements set in "Plan" – not, did you remember to do some testing. The required level of improvement should not be forgotten; it should be achieved (or exceeded) by the new proposed way of working.

Within "Pick up the pen game" you learnt to measure how effective the trials were; did they represent the process (compare like with like) and did they deliver the original requirement (compare results against goal)?

Chapter 6 teaches you to check that the process delivers the original goals. It also checks that the process is easy to follow and is not unpredictable in time, effort and output. It even asked you not to be scared in going back to repeat some work.

Principle 9: Build consensus

You want to ensure that everyone agrees that the new solution should be implemented.

Within "Pick up the pen game" you learnt that if you have a simple, clear solution to a problem, which does not need consensus outside the empowered group, go ahead.

Chapter 6 teaches you to work with all colleagues on the new solution that has been found. If you need to check with even one other person, share the problem, share your insight and build consensus.

As you are building a learning organization you will beat the competition when you properly apply "Check". Therefore you will need to go through every activity you have completed to date, starting with the problem and

What problem are you trying to solve?

answering every question, until all colleagues agree whether or not the solution works.

Please do not forget to encourage and reward people who take a chance and use their brains; this started with setting them meaningful goals in **PRINCIPLE 2**, and should now result in unanimous agreement to either act by implementing the new standard or to act by revisiting earlier principles.

What problem are you trying to solve?

CHAPTER 7: "ACT" BY IMPLEMENTING

Establish the new standard

PRINCIPLE 10

You have tested and proven the solution. You also have a good suggestion on how to follow the process (or the trials would not work). You now need to implement with the **10TH PRINCIPLE** and establish a new standard.

As the solution is now the proven best way to perform this process, it should be easy to build consensus around the standard that is being proposed. Again use your empowered group and include colleagues that are trusted by anyone that will be asked to follow the standard; as whenever a standard exists, and you want the benefits of continuous improvement on it, the standard must be followed. You need to avoid all excuses to not follow the new standard.

The team should aim to make sure that the new standard is covering five perspectives;
1. Ownership is with the people being asked to follow the new standard.
2. That it has simple and visual descriptions.
3. That it is easy to train and follow.
4. That it accurately describes the expected output.
5. That a relevant measure can show everyone this is a better process.

Overall, it should be simple to understand but not made simple.

What problem are you trying to solve?

A tidy garage

A good Standard Operating Procedure (SOP) (or even a standardized work Diagram) will properly cover all perspectives a good standard requires; the steps of the process will be properly described, key points for any person following the process are identified and the briefest possible descriptions are used to ensure success when using the process (think Lego instruction manuals).

Excess information on these diagrams / procedures proliferates easily. You need to remember you are trying to have standards for the core processes in everyone's job. The diagrams / procedures only need to be a standard, when people need them to share / use / store their core processes. The standards on the diagrams / procedures in your organization are not about making it easy for process guardians to say "every diagram / procedure looks the same, so they must be working". You are not improving a process so you can achieve ISO certification; you are doing it to ensure you remove too much effort.

As a picture speaks a thousand words, so does an example. An SOP is the standard you want everyone to follow when operating the process (and continue / build upon the benefits achieved when adopting the standard).

The following example will therefore concentrate on "using the garage" not "maintaining the standard". Of course I would never suggest you go and tidy your garage, unless you have a problem you are trying to solve and standardized work is potentially a good solution to that problem.

What problem are you trying to solve?

THE JOY OF STANDARDS / PAGE 123

DIAGRAM X: A slightly excessive standard on how to use the garage

LOCATION OF STANDARD: On back door to garage (A)	REASON FOR STANDARD (B): 1 hour less cleaning / gardening every week: as we don't have to search to find things and go back and forth to / from the garage during a chore – we can select all the required equipment with much less effort	DATE STANDARD TO BE REVIEWED: 21st June 2016 (C)

ACTIVITY	DESCRIPTION	DETAILS TO SUCCEED
1) Ensure garage is clean, safe and ready to use	Review the cleaning log (D) (below this standard). If the last cleaning was more than 10 days ago, complete the 3 minute cleaning routine.	3 minute cleaning routine 1. Get cleaning materials (ZONE 4) 2. Dust and inspect for 60 seconds 3. Sweep floor for 60 seconds
2) Go to your item	A) Follow the zoning guide (E) [Zone layout: Garage opening on left, Back Door on right. ZONE 1 Car, ZONE 2 Dad's tools, ZONE 3 Everyday tools, ZONE 4 Cleaning, ZONE 5 Sports equipment, ZONE 6 Gardening. Center: KEEP CLEAR FOR CAR]	
	B) Find your item by using the checklist next to each zone	ZONE 1 (CAR) Location 1 = Shampoo Location 2 = Bucket Location 3 = Sponge Location 4 = Oil
3) Leave the garage tidy	RETURN everything. REORDER what is needed. REMEMBER to update the measures.	

KEY TO DIAGRAM X:

(A) So everyone can see before they enter the garage (when they get something).

(B) So everyone will want to follow the standard.

(C) No owner, approver, date created in this example: it's a garage not a nuclear power station.

(D) Opportunity for a measure? Also did you find what you wanted? Was it ready for use? Did you buy something and find you already had one.

(E) Zoned for ease of use: Everyday items next to back door, car wash & heavy garden items next to garage opening.

What problem are you trying to solve?

A car without a petrol gauge

A process without a measure is like a car without a petrol gauge, it tells you something just at the wrong time. So identify the right measures that you need to support the process and avoid the embarrassing and inconvenient breakdowns.

First you need to understand why you are having the measure. What problem will it solve? What will it identify? Is it worth tracking? Or should your people just highlight facts within their established routines?

Then ensure the measure is relevant to the people that are being asked to complete the measure and let them choose the easiest way to complete the measure. Is it a plain piece of paper with a pen, collected daily which will tally what needs to be counted or is it something that can be readily taken from a computer system?

As an improving measure usually indicates an improving process, ensure that there is a target or trend expectation for the measure; you have to ensure that you will act on the measure, is it that after 20 errors you will attack the most frequent problem? Or is it that if you only complete 100 today, you will ask everyone to suggest what could be improved, so more can be completed?

Lastly, every measure should be almost effort free to produce, completed by someone within the process and visible to everyone. If you do not empower the people within the process to manage and disclose performance / issues, then why should you expect them to be improving the process?

What problem are you trying to solve?

THE JOY OF STANDARDS / PAGE 125

Train the new standard

PRINCIPLE 11

You need to follow some fundamentals when training the new standard. It is worth realizing that failing to train the new standard, in an effective and definite manner, is almost as bad as failing to optimize a process with standardized work. This fundamental requirement should ensure answers to the following questions.

WHAT SHOULD BE USED TO TRAIN PEOPLE?
The Standard Operating Procedure (SOP) with some speaker notes and participant notes. Enough training material to; ensure people are able to complete the process in the recommended time and to the recommended specifications (quality).

WHEN SHOULD TRAINING BE CONDUCTED AND FOR HOW LONG?
Just before someone is expected to follow the process; either a new starter or an existing employee (adopting a revised process). Avoid; train, forget, then go-live.

There is no set rule on how long to train someone. For tasks which require dexterous abilities (physical tasks) practice the process until employees are able to perform the task without fumbling, using the wrong sequence or producing a defect.

For tasks which require cognitive abilities (information tasks) practice the process until employees are confident that they can produce the process most of the time, the trainer should then be available over the coming days to support any questions.

What problem are you trying to solve?

WHO SHOULD CONDUCT THE TRAINING AND WHEN?

Someone who is an expert, a manager or someone from within the process should conduct the training. Only credible people will be accepted by those being trained as fully understanding everything that needs to be taught.

HOW AND WHERE SHOULD TRAINING BE CONDUCTED?

Provide the training in a protected environment, with simulated demands from customers, close to the workplace. Follow a series of training methods which facilitate demonstration, explanation and practice. Avoid excuses that the training was artificial or that the training facility was strange or difficult to attend. Try creating a training facility near the workplace – even the manager's office can be forsaken (for example: I have seen a manager give up their office so their people had a training room).

WHAT BENEFITS ARISE FROM BETTER TRAINING?

Your standards are kept up-to-date when they are used in training. Standards are kept relevant to all employees as when a new employee is trained the trainer needs to check that the training material is suitable for them.

I have seen an employee trained in 2 weeks instead of 3 months, giving the organization 11 more weeks of productive time, this is an undeniable benefit.

Other benefits of good training / good training materials are that you will have the knowledge in the walls of your organization not in the legs of your people. When someone leaves, their knowledge of the process does not leave.

You will also find that you start employing and hiring people with the right behaviors and attitude, rather than trying to find the elusive perfectly skilled person. This results in lower salary costs in your organization as you are able

What problem are you trying to solve?

to bring people in, train them quickly (to perform at levels never previously dreamed) and use their brains not just their hands.

This is in fact the opposite of the question asked earlier in **DIAGRAM K:** Proposed reasons for high or low performance. With effective training you can swap the phrase "reasons for high or low performance" with "reasons for high or low payroll costs".

Although widely accepted as a great way to run your organization, training is still poorly managed and poorly delivered by most. I have had the privilege of working in organizations which take training seriously, but still find it hard to find an optimum method.

Looking at history, I can find one outstanding training example, it is based on Charles R. Allen's early 20th century work; it is the simple and effective "Training Within Industry" program. In the early 1940s the USA was faced with a shortage of workers in farming and heavy industry. Their answer was to instantly create thousands of trainers with a set of guides called: Job Instruction, Job Method and Job Relations instruction cards. These ensured that they could quickly train people to cover skilled worker positions. They discovered a simple and effective solution to the **11TH PRINCIPLE**. My challenge for you is to discover the same simplicity in your training requirements for your new standards.

What problem are you trying to solve?

Manage the new standard

PRINCIPLE 12

Continuous improvement happens when PDCA (through standardized work) is followed by SDCA (Standardize-Do-Check-Act) to implement and manage standards. **PRINCIPLES 10 & 11** have already started to handle "Standardize" and "Do". You now need to manage the solution to fully achieve the Joy of Standards; how will you check that it is working and how will you act to improve it?

DIAGRAM Y: PDCA and its continuous relationship with SDCA

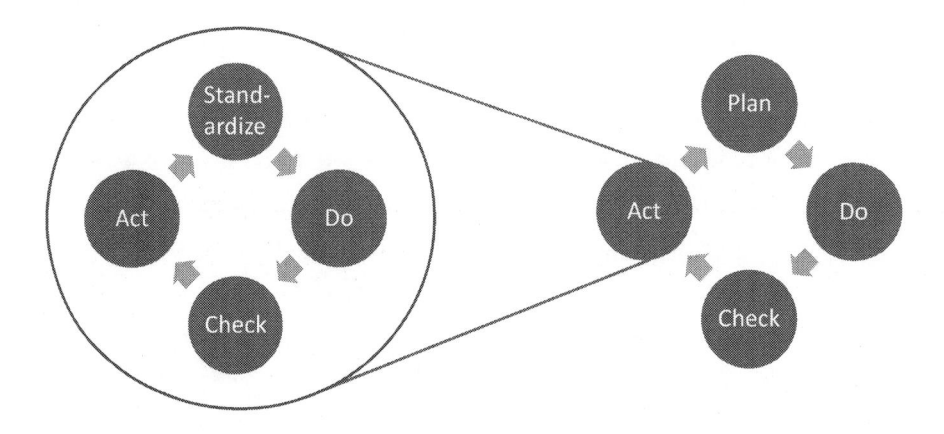

The diagram above shows that every time you run a PDCA cycle and reach "Act" you start a SDCA cycle. Complimentarily, every time you run a SDCA cycle and reach "Act" you can trigger a PDCA cycle. This trigger is not always guaranteed, this is why you need **PRINCIPLE 12** to manage and challenge the new standard.

What problem are you trying to solve?

When acting to implement and manage the standard, you need to ensure SDCA:

"STANDARDIZE" THE WAY THAT THE PROCESS IS PERFORMED
- Follow **PRINCIPLE 10** and establish the new standard in a relevant, communicative and pragmatic way.
- Follow **PRINCIPLE 11** and train the right people in an effective way. Do not waste everyone's time with either excessive or inadequate training.

"DO" THE PROCESS EVERY TIME THAT THE ACTIVITY NEEDS TO BE COMPLETED (EXCEPTIONS TO THIS TELLS YOU THERE IS A PROBLEM)
- Require everyone to follow the standard every day that the process is to be completed; a quickly improving standard needs to be checked every day.
- Ensure that people have someone to go to if they have a question (an expert* or trainer); who will someone go to for help or do you want them to stop using the standard?
- Ensure that people have someone to go to if the process will not deliver what the customer wants (this is called a help chain, something which will respond quickly); problems happen, look at the bumper stickers on the back of cars. They will happen less, now that you have an easy and relevant way to perform the process to the right quality, speed and effort – but you should not forget that problems happen and when they do, your people need to be able to go to someone to help them solve the problem.

*experts are still needed, but their roles are different when performing standards under the SDCA cycle, they no longer put out fires, they prevent them.

What problem are you trying to solve?

"Check" that the process is Followed and is meeting the expected performance levels for effort, leadtime and quality

- No process can always deliver what the customer wants. Sometimes you need to evolve the standard to reflect adapting customer needs, only checking that the process is followed will discover this.
- Ensure people use the Standard Operating Procedure to help them perform the process (every day that they perform the process); following the latest procedure is more relevant than following a dusty memory.
- Ensure that the measure / opportunity to discuss performance of the process is regularly updated (every day is a good starting point); it ensures you can "Act" on a daily basis and have a process which people can follow.
- Ensure that you count how often problems happen; otherwise how will you know which are the common problems which need to be solved in "Act"?

If something went wrong, then you and your sponsor need to learn lessons for the future. Learn how to act quickly to ensure that the new standard is kept effective; otherwise people will stop using it.

Reward people for showing you when the standard is not working and encourage them to do something positive about it. You should never punish people for showing you or telling you that they do not follow the standard. You have learnt something valuable; do not fail them now by punishing them for a revelation which tells you to fix the standard, make a new conclusion:

If their process is not being followed, something went wrong with your process!

What problem are you trying to solve?

Either something has changed or something has failed in one or more of your earlier principles:

PRINCIPLE 1: was the wrong group of people empowered?
PRINCIPLE 2: was the wrong goal for improvement chosen?
PRINCIPLE 3: were the ways of working not properly understood?
PRINCIPLE 4: was a poor sequence for the task chosen?
PRINCIPLE 5: was a poor workplace layout chosen?
PRINCIPLE 6: was poor visual management chosen?
PRINCIPLE 7: was the test giving misleading results?
PRINCIPLE 8: was the evaluation against the goals and checking of the previous principles too superficial and / or did it ignore relevant evidence?
PRINCIPLE 9: was consensus not achieved with the right people?
PRINCIPLE 10: was the new standard not established sustainably?
PRINCIPLE 11: was the training material or training approach ineffective?

"ACT" ON OPPORTUNITIES TO IMPROVE THE PROCESS
- Ensure that problems are systematically investigated and resolved; this is about making the process work for all of the stakeholders. Your people are your most important participants they are your eyes and ears.
- Ensure that the process is kept up-to-date with regular review; there is an owner, who agrees to review the process at least yearly and maybe even monthly (on a regularly used process by many people).
- Consider launching the next standardized work PDCA cycle, when the opportunity arises, there is always more waste in a process to tackle.

This list of SDCA suggestions may seem long but you need to professionally manage the solution. You need to encourage a process which is always followed and every opportunity for improvement is taken. You do not want any of the benefits for the customers, employees and organization to slowly slip away and erode competitiveness.

Ultimately, you do not want to follow performance levels shown in **DIAGRAM A** (left hand diagram = PDCA without SDCA) as you want the high performing process shown in **DIAGRAM B** (right hand diagram = SDCA & PDCA in perfect harmony).

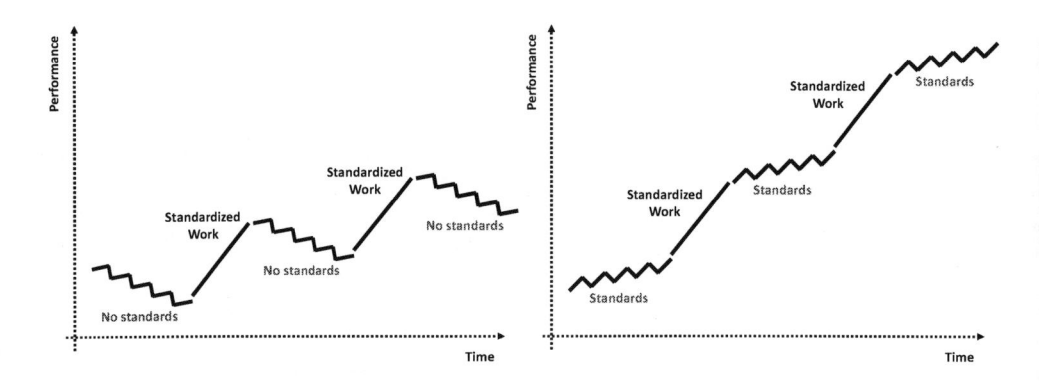

What problem are you trying to solve?

Want to know a secret?

You may think that this is the craziest, most illogical thing I could say: Audit your people as part of SDCA "Check". See with your own eyes that they are following the process. Why on earth would you do something like this? You have empowered them, they have found a solution, they have tested, they have adopted, they have been trained, they even have routines to monitor and improve the process. So why audit them?

Managers have a duty to show their people that they care:

- If you ask your people to follow a process and refer to the Standard Operating Procedure daily – are you there, standing beside them whilst they complete their process, on a regular basis – to show them how important their work is and to encourage them to follow and improve standards? Have you ever watched an employee performing a process? Have you been looking at the Standard Operating Procedure to see if they have been following the standard? Have you ever asked them why they were not following the standard; were they not trained properly, is the process out of date, is the process not capable of following the correct customer demands or have they found a better way to perform the process?

- If you ask your people to meet every day* and discuss how the process is performing – are you going to some of these meetings on a regular basis – to show how proud you are of their achievements? How about to encourage the next level of improvement or the next process to improve?

What problem are you trying to solve?

*Every day as a work week involves more than one day; if one employee is missing one day, some work will need to be reallocated – a weekly or monthly meeting will never be able to cope with the variety of circumstances that people (not robots) experience on a daily basis. The same happens with customer and organization requirements; these can change at a frequency which is faster than weekly or monthly. Leadership is about getting people to follow you, as a team, in achieving your organizational goals; if you run your organization as though every day counts, then get your people to meet daily. If you do not, then competitors that meet daily will beat you.

Both of these recommendations for audit are opportunities to coach employees to be more successful and to encourage even more continuous improvement. None of these are opportunities to manage someone for poor performance (unless you want to encourage people to hide things from you).

This duty to stop managing people and start coaching them is for a reason. Let your organization be the one that is consistently delivering to customers, beating the competition, delighting employees and giving shareholders top and bottom line growth, through the power of your people.

There is some guidance for time to be spent on the PDCA and SDCA cycles. This is sometimes given as 10% of everyone's time. I like to split this to 5% on each of the two subjects. That is around 2 hours per employee and per manager each week on PDCA and 2 hours each week on SDCA.

How to spend your time on the PDCA and SDCA cycles:
- 2 hours PDCA employee time will be an average across all employees in any particular week – ideally with every employee (including management), every month, in at least one PDCA activity.

What problem are you trying to solve?

- Managers should also spend additional time sponsoring and encouraging PDCA with meaningful goals which challenge and improve processes.
- 2 hours SDCA employee time will be every employee in their daily review (10-15 minutes every day) and their constant incremental improvement of standards.
- 2 hours SDCA manager time will be the same as every employee. The difference here is that managers have different standards to follow, for example: a manager visiting a team's daily review is part of management Standard Operating Procedure.

I mentioned that I have seen an organization where the manager donated their office for training purposes, in this organization I have seen the Chief Executive Officer listed as a trainer (leading by example and showing that every manager should master PDCA and SDCA so they can teach and coach PDCA and SDCA). He is also checking that the restaurant is conducting daily reviews and even inspecting the standards that are followed in the process (printing them out, watching the employee and having a constructive discussion with them afterwards). A great example if I also reveal that 15 years ago they had one customer in one country, their customer went bankrupt, but they did not – they had diversified and are now present in over 100 countries with over 10,000 staff. This is evidence of an organization that knows how to do both PDCA and SDCA.

What problem are you trying to solve?

The key in a keystroke

Having a conversation with a customer service manager, it became clear to me that the auditing of the standard was not seen as advantageous. I challenged the manager to come with me and see how it works. We immediately sat down next to a customer service clerk and asked them to follow the new standard.

The employee opened their ERP system (SAP) and typed a date as follows:

DD.MM.YYYY

I asked the manager if they had ever seen anyone do the date differently, they said yes, some people do the date format as follows:

DDMMYY

As SAP autocorrects and improves the date to the required format.

So by observing an employee once, the manager was now able to coach the employee to improve the standard (for everyone in the team) and use the new way of inputting the date. This new way of inputting the date was 4 keystrokes quicker, for 100 items a day for 20 people for 150 days a year. That is a saving of 1.2 million key strokes a year in a team of 20 people, 2000 people work on similar processes, the potential is 100 fold. This is how a manager becomes a leader, encouraging people to improve standards, through observation of followed standards.

REFLECT: SDCA is not Still-Don't-Change-Anything and that includes leadership styles on leading people and encouraging improvement.

What problem are you trying to solve?

Summary of Principles that "Act"

If you can answer the following statements with conviction (remember **CHAPTER 1**), then you can say you are on the path to continuous improvement:

- People are being trained and coached in application of the new standard.
- Leaders are ensuring that the new standard is adhered to.
- People are taking action to improve the process when problems or opportunities are being detected.

These statements are ensured by following **PRINCIPLES 10, 11 AND 12**.

PRINCIPLE 10: ESTABLISH THE NEW STANDARD
You want to ensure that you create a process which can be followed by everyone.

Within "Pick up the pen game" you learnt to always make the simplest Standard Operating Procedure you can possibly make; and to re-use everything you can from process trials, including timing, if this helps to deliver an accurate standard.

Chapter 7 teaches you that you need to remember why the process was being optimized. The standard must implement a process that supports the original goal, not something else; a simple visual way to follow the standard must be invented and kept in a prominent position to remind everyone to follow it. You also discovered the importance of establishing a measure to support the process; something to highlight performance, issues or opportunities.

What problem are you trying to solve?

Principle 11: Train the New Standard

You want to ensure that the new standard is trained in the most effective way possible.

Within "Pick up the pen game" you learnt that training does not have to be complicated. Training just has to be effective and relevant. The key is to find solutions which concentrate on the fundamentals within the process.

Chapter 7 teaches you to find a respected trainer, a suitable training method, a suitable location and to learn with actual or simulated demands. Train to the level needed to have success and provide support to your people when they have questions when using the standard.

You also learnt to look to the past and consider how Training Within Industry (TWI) may be relevant to the training hurdles you face today.

Principle 12: Manage the New Standard

You want to ensure that the new standard is given a level of care and attention that shows that management supports the use of the new standard. You do not want the process to fall back into the old ways; you want it to continuously improve for the benefit of all stakeholders.

Within "Pick up the pen game" you learnt to show people that the original objective (and therefore the solution) was meaningful and follow through any request to follow a new process with direct management support.

Chapter 7 teaches you that managers need to ensure they are "caring to coach" by attending daily gatherings that discuss the process and that they watch employees follow the new standards. This is not a breach of trust, it is

What problem are you trying to solve?

a statement of unequivocal support which must be in place. You do not want the new standard to fail.

Ultimately, you want to ensure that the process is continuously improving. You learnt that this will be the result of excellent leadership from start to finish on **PRINCIPLES 1 TO 12**. This is not a task for leaders to delegate, this is the Joy of Standards.

What problem are you trying to solve?

CONCLUSION

Banish reductionism

The 12 principles described in the Joy of Standards are ruthless in eliminating waste **Diagram C** (left) and even have the potential to create more value for your customers **Diagram D** (right).

Heads or Tails?

Remove waste to be reliable

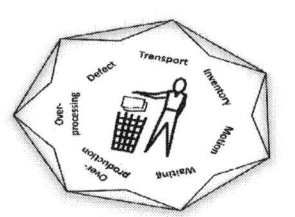

Heads or Tails?

Create value in the eyes of the customer

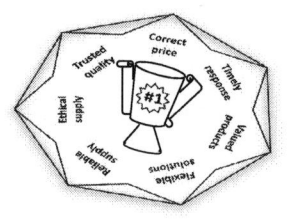

However, this is not where your story ends, but where your story should begin. Many organizations fail to grasp the reality of what to do with the released capacity when making the transition through the Joy of Standards. Released capacity needs to be used (sold to customers), failure to use spare capacity is almost as bad as failure to improve the standard. Therefore these are the recommended ways to use this spare capacity for growth purposes.

Growth Strategy #1: Use your existing people and their spare time to sell more products (and produce more products). This works when your competition does not adjust and you have room to take more market share. However, if your competition does adjust or your market share is at saturation point, then you will only make small progress with this growth strategy.

What problem are you trying to solve?

Growth Strategy #2: Use your existing people and their spare time to be creative and to discover more products and services which will expand your product offering and help you to stay ahead of the innovation pipeline. This "Google time" (every Friday is available to any employee to do anything they like) is not as focused as some may want but, let's be honest, can produce some fantastic results. I have even seem a team of "creative" people adopt the Joy of Standards in one week and deliver a permanent 20% spare capacity the following week. This was after years of complaining that there was no time to do self-determined projects and only time to do core-business projects.

Growth Strategy #3: Do the opposite of your competition: make the market place yours with mass customization and intense product support.

Most organizations today are concentrating on slimming down their product offerings and going for economies of scale. This shrinking to greatness strategy is a reaction to failed economies of scale (which tried to exist without standards). Now that you have the Joy of Standards you could also follow this path. But are you missing something, could the capacity be used differently?

Mass customization is now an option, your people are in control of their standards and therefore can afford to take on more variety (if it is a good growth driver). Good variety is difficult to define, until you look at the 7 values in the eyes of the customer. Do not add variety to your processes or their inputs, instead, add variety to your products. BMW is able to offer millions of variations of the same model, not because it customizes its processes, but because it customizes its offering.

Your competition will be scratching its head, how can they do this, they must be cheating; this was the true meaning of the Lean books like "The machine that changed the world", "Lean Thinking" and "The Toyota Way". High

What problem are you trying to solve?

variety / low cost is possible, even within large organizations, when they have the Joy of Standards.

Last but not least, intense product support. Premium service / relevant cost is possible. This iPhone or Amazon factor killed Nokia and bookstores. The business landscape has changed since the beginning of the millennium, the digital age is disrupting the market place. Apple offers intense product experiences and intense product support whilst selling a very standardized product. They have introduced value (rather than reducing cost) and invested in a growth strategy which killed the competition. Amazon is no different, next day delivery and millions of titles is an unbeatable proposition when the book arrives at your doorstep without you having to go to the shops (for less availability and less variety). Amazon now wants to be the world's largest grocer, a true growth strategy is being followed.

My advice is to leverage the Joy of Standard by embracing the customer if you want to grow. Invest your released capacity into customer experience and customized offerings. Intense product support, chocolate bar by chocolate bar delivery to people's homes and workplaces is possible, when you have the insight to invest spare capacity into growth opportunities. Every large organization lists small organizations as agile. Every small organization lists large organizations as having an unfair economy of scale. With the Joy of standards, every organization can be jealous of your organization.

What problem are you trying to solve?

A letter from John Shook

On 11th June 2015, I received a letter from John Shook, Chairman and CEO of Lean Enterprise Institute Inc. I have reproduced this letter which is entitled Work. A question I asked myself (and you can also ask): Is this letter another justification for the Joy of Standards?

"*Dear James,*

We need to think about redefining work. Until we – anyone who wishes to bring about organizational change – redefine the actual value-creating work of the business, we haven't made any changes that are meaningful. You may be able to create wealth through a variety of business models or ways of thinking. But if you want to create real value, and jobs that value people, you must think hard about how your people are working every day. That's because the essence of lean thinking is about the WORK. Lean means working on the work: the value-creating work that occurs on the frontlines of your enterprise."

If you want me as your employee to give you my heart and soul, then consider whether the work is menial or meaningful. Will I do that if the relationship we have is one of a mere monetary transaction? There's nothing morally wrong with a purely transactional relationship, if that's our mutual agreement. But if you want me and each person in your organization to fully commit, we need to be aligned on purpose. Aligned on why we are here, on what we are trying to accomplish. Then, I can focus – applying all my humanity – on the work in front of me, the work at hand.

What problem are you trying to solve?

I am outraged at the comments I hear so prevalently nowadays – "We know how to do the work, we just need to change our culture." Or, "We know the lean tools, we want the lean culture." Or any assumption that people can become engaged in continuous improvement as a training exercise. This way of thinking is all-too-often paired with vague claims that, "Oh, we engage our people. People are the most important part of the process. We just turn them loose and they take ownership of their own work ...."

Really? Your people decided that the coffee shop is located above the subway station and needs to open every day at 5:00 a.m.? They decided to be the only trauma center within 200 miles? They decided that the new building will be constructed in a swamp? They decided that their worth is $20 per hour?

Each person comes to work every day and does a job. In an office, on an assembly line. In the C-suite, at the reception desk. Out on a construction site, in a cube farm. Doing heart surgery, brewing coffee. Lean thinking asks: What IS the work?? And what is care and feeding of that work? Who does that care and feeding? How?? So let's not fool ourselves and each other with talk of "meaningful work". Of "our people are our most valuable resource". Of "respect for people". We cannot have this conversation without a deep respect for both the people and the work itself.

Is your work menial or meaningful? How about both? It's okay for meaningful work to appear menial. Most of most work days consist of exactly that, no matter how glamorous it may look from the outside. Talk to a surgeon at the end of her long day in the operating room. Is it good work??

Unfortunately, many purported advocates of meaningful work are the quickest to demean labor. For example, working on the assembly line. Note the underlying assumption of the common observation, "That job is like working on an assembly line ...."

_{*What problem are you trying to solve?*}

If the assembly line is demeaning, then let's get rid of it. You, then, Ms. Consumer, can pick up the price tag and pay the penalty of poor quality that will come from people trying to hand-build – which is mainly, you know, a process full of rework in the name of craftsmanship: "Let me shave off just a little more here, oh, too much, now I'll have to shave off some more over here ...."

I'm not saying craftsmanship isn't real – I'm saying if it is real and a good thing, then let's elevate all work to that level and give it the respect it deserves.

Making things is in its essential nature a meaningful thing. It is among the most meaningful of the many ways we humans can choose to fill our time. Factory work – whether job shop or assembly line, carving picture frames or fabricating steering brackets – is a way we organize ourselves to make things. It is immensely rewarding, meaningful work. Or it can be if we choose.

So, let's make it so. Let's elevate the work. Celebrate it. And, with that, let's treat it – the work – with the deep respect it deserves. That applies to the lowly receptionist. Or the more respected surgeon. Or a street sweeper.

Lean thinking is about, more than anything else, rethinking, reimagining what work can be. To do so, we have to start with the purpose of the work. We ask "Why are we doing this, what problem are we trying to solve?" You, as the owner or CEO, have a problem you are trying to solve, which has brought you to this position of gathering together dozens or thousands of individuals on a daily basis to do this work, to create this value together.

I had the dispiriting experience recently of walking the gemba with a young entrepreneur, a Lean Startup aficionado, who explained to me how his system

_{What problem are you trying to solve?}

design was perfect and the only problem was that he couldn't get good workers who would operate it properly. I couldn't believe my ears. Pressing him, he emphasized, "No, we just can't get good workers around here."

It was a picking operation. Many items were out of place because the pickers would sometimes mistakenly pick the wrong part, then set it back in an incorrect location.

We walked and talked and I left his gemba with a profound sense of personal failure that I could not find the words to show him an alternative way to think about his situation. He actually thought he had the perfect business system, one he was confident would soon (and probably will) bring him great wealth (despite, by the way, the horrible customer service); his problem was bad workers.

Contrast that with this. Build your business from the work. Define the work based on the value you will provide the customer, on the work to be done to solve the customer's problem. Build the work (the business) from there so that whoever (I intentionally avoid here the word that makes so many uncomfortable: "the worker") is doing the work can do it perfectly every time. When a customer asks for his favorite beverage, the barista knows how to do the work to provide it. And when the inevitable problem arises – "Oh, more customers than we've ever had at this time of day …!" – he/she knows how to (1) observe that there is a problem, (2) devise a quick response to make the immediate situation better, (3) come up with some ideas for making the situation better next time, and (4) how to give those ideas a try and judge how well they worked.

And, here's the kicker, the real reward: he/she knows that while that particular problem will not occur again, he/she is completely comfortable knowing that another problem, a different problem, absolutely WILL occur.

What problem are you trying to solve?

Probably very soon – "It's okay, I will deal with each situation as it arises, as a new challenge to keep making things better and better."

And here's an even bigger kicker: rather than wait on the next problem, he/she will create it! By learning to see "problems" merely as "gaps" between the way things are now versus the way they should or could be, we can start to see every situation as a problem waiting to be solved. For example, when the barista fine tunes the size of batches of brewed coffee, or does away with batches entirely by going to a pour-over method for each cup, or challenges the team to respond even more quickly when lines begin to form during peak times of the day. Problems no longer reside in the realm of things that happen to us; they are improvements-in-waiting, gaps we can tackle as part and parcel of doing our regular work.

Back to that street sweeper, consider this by Martin Luther King: If a man is called to be a street sweeper, he should sweep streets even as a Michelangelo painted, or Beethoven composed music or Shakespeare wrote poetry. He should sweep streets so well that all the hosts of heaven and earth will pause to say, "Here lived a great street sweeper who did his job well."

So, these ideals – "Let's make work meaningful" – aren't new. What is new are the means to make work meaningful through lean thinking.

John Shook
Chairman and CEO
Lean Enterprise Institute, Inc.
jshook@lean.org

P. S. A key element for respecting the work is proper coaching."

What problem are you trying to solve?

Standards work

I have had the privilege of working with people in 4 continents when implementing standards and standardized work. Two things have never failed to amaze me.

The first is that opportunities exist everywhere and can be found by anyone. You think seven(ty) percent is too much effort to remove from a process, I think that sevent(ty) percent should be the annual goal. If we fail, this is okay. If we fail to try, this is the real problem.

The second amazing thing is that people never ever fail to surprise me. I worked in business for over 15 years before I saw continuous improvement; I managed people following broken processes. I now live in awe of people who make changes to their processes, their jobs and their lives. These people embrace lean thinking, they have been waiting for it all their lives and the Joy of Standards is the perfect step towards a truly satisfying role.

This is all about managing processes to become better and better for the benefit of all stakeholders. I explained earlier that there are three versions of processes:
1. What you think the process is (based on memory).
2. What it actually is (observation of today's process).
3. What it should be (optimum which should be followed).

Standards ensure that items 1 and 2 are the same thing. Standardized work brings a process to its full potential from item 2 to item 3.

What problem are you trying to solve?

The **12 Principles** will take you to joyful standards which deliver something beneficial for the customer, the employee and your organization. These win-win situations do not happen outside lean thinking. Forget one or two of your stakeholders for the blinkered view of a few (taking the non-lean option will always be, for almost everyone, the default without standardized work).

Let the principles guide you, challenge you and suggest a lean option which delivers for all of your stakeholders.

Principles that **"Plan"**	1st Empower a group of people
	2nd Establish a goal for improvement
Principles that **"Do"**	3rd Understand the ways of working
	4th Find a better sequence for the task
	5th Make the workplace easy
	6th Find a great way to follow the task
Principles that **"Check"**	7th Test the proposed way of working
	8th Evaluate the test
	9th Build consensus
Principles that **"Act"**	10th Establish the new standard
	11th Train the new standard
	12th Manage the new standard

You do all of this to implement both sides of the lean thinking strategy: **Heads** (be flexible to create value) and **Tails** (remove waste to be reliable).

What problem are you trying to solve?

As a result you eliminate process variation and create predictable effort within processes and reliable output. Most (or sometimes even all) variants of the process are delivered with an empowered group of people who will take the process from its challenge in **PRINCIPLE 2** through to its implementation in **PRINCIPLES 10 TO 12**.

With clearly understood processes, which have defined roles and trained employees, focused on following the standard operating procedure, monitoring performance and suggesting improvement continuously has ensured that broken processes have become a thing of the past.

Consequences of this improvement is every leader's dream; higher customer satisfaction, increased employee engagement and profitable growth for the organization. I say this is every leader's dream but I still wonder why, over 100 years after Henry Ford invented the moving production line, it is not every leader's reality?

What problem are you trying to solve?

Coming soon

If your organization is finding it hard to deliver consistent high quality then this book is your lifeline. Many organizations believe that the answer to excessive structural costs is to trim the fat. Lean has a different answer; fix the processes and lead them forward with appropriate measures. You no longer have to be a rocket scientist to manage your organization, all you have to do is Rethink Quality & Measures.

Prevent errors and avoid defects:

RETHINK QUALITY & MEASURES

The first ever book on how to create a high quality organization without the high effort. Insightful measurement with pragmatic quality based improvement; a must for every organization that wants to deliver its promises.

What problem are you trying to solve?

About the author

I spent the first 5 years of my career becoming a qualified accountant; auditing around 100 enterprises from the retail, wholesale, service and manufacturing industries. Enjoyment came from being in a team, creating a solution and training others. Reflection tells me I was looking in the business rear view mirror.

I spent the next 5 years of my career as a management accountant working on management reporting, business planning and systems implementation. I had moved from the rear view mirror to the dashboard, but I was not driving the car.

I also spent 5 years as a financial controller; I thought I was the driver. In business terms I was the co-pilot (the finance function contributes to the business effectiveness; it does not usually generate revenue or facilitate customer products).

Then my perspective changed, I became a lean coach and completed a master's degree in Lean Operations. Finally I see myself as a driving instructor; helping people learn how to navigate the business tests thrown at them. All this would not be possible without people. All the people I have had the pleasure to work and study with; the time and patience that they have given me will never be forgotten. Questions are welcome, knowledge is to be shared not horded, please feel free to contact me on LinkedIn.

James Sandfield **FCCA MSc**
January 2016

What problem are you trying to solve?